THINK IT

— PITCH IT —

SELL IT

by

Pierre-Lewis Coombes

First paperback edition April 2021

Book cover design by Faaizah Sinnappudu
edited and proofread by Kelly George
Book Design and Format by Bilal sha

www.thinkpitchsell.com

ACKNOWLEDGMENTS

To my younger self, the dyslexic, creative lost soul who dreamt of pop stardom but fell into sales, you did something with your life!

To my Mum & Dad, sister, grandparent-ts, to my family here and no longer but still in memory, thank you for being there and for the many memories.

Thank you to everyone I've worked with, both as colleagues and as clients, for being part of my continuing journey.

In the creation of this book thank you to my editor and proof-reader, Kelly George and for the cover artwork Faaizah Sinnappudu.

To my baby boy Xavier, if you ever read this when you are older, I hope it makes you proud, and there is some bit of me in the words that you can hold forever and pass on. Equally, I hope you can learn from some of the lessons, ideas, and tips in this book. Daddy loves you more than he could ever put into words.

And lastly, with every quantum piece of my being, thank you to the most incredible partner, mum, and lady. Thank you, Paige. I Love you more than I can explain. Thank you for putting up with my madness, introverted ways, occasional grumpiness, and thoughtful silence and for allowing me to follow my soul in business and creative ventures such as this.

TABLE OF CONTENTS

Introduction 1

I've been there before. 4

Who are they? 18

A leap of faith 30

Standing on their shoulders 36

Selling on the phone 42

Sweet music on the harp of Dublin 68

Words to sell by 86

A little inspiration 98

Tellers of the secret future 109

Another crossroads 123

Closed deal 133

Thank you 140

TABLE OF CONTENTS

INTRODUCTION

*H*ave you ever thought of an idea and wanted to make it happen but doubted yourself? Perhaps you have a new or small business and need to work out a sales strategy? Maybe you're looking for guidance, don't have direction and want to learn some practical tools, techniques, and concepts to help you figure life out. This is the book for you!

I've wanted to write a book for the best part of four years now, but each time I started, within a chapter or two, I stopped. Each time I didn't have an ultimate direction for a book, it always came to a crashing halt until it hit me.

I thought long and hard, and as the pandemic came and as things closed down, I reflected. The change of direction and the new normal got me thinking. I found myself in a similar introverted mindset to when I first started my business many years ago.

I spoke to several people who had lost their jobs and been affected by the downward economic spiral. I saw many new businesses and people deciding to change their lives, like the flowers that grow so vibrantly out of dying century-old trees, fallen after a violent storm.

As the founder of Big Wolf Marketing, a group of lead generation companies, I've worked with many start-ups and small businesses to help them with their sales. I have even given some strategic advice and direction. I very often get determined individuals reaching out to me as a 'Sales and marketing expert.' They may have seen me online at a talk or on TV for advice and support. Yet, due to time restraints and the scheduled work we have within our agencies, I'm unable to give them the compassionate ear and helping hand I would like to.

I decided to write this book to help all the many new business owners, budding entrepreneurs, and small businesses, wanting advice, selling their ideas and their product and services.

This semi-autobiographical story is just that a 'story,' yet written from experience. In any situation that directly reflects real life, I've made sure to change names, swap places, conceal various elements in the interest of confidentiality and be discreet.

I've embedded many sales tips, tricks, and techniques and given advice on marketing strategies for businesses wanting to generate more sales. Whether you are thinking of starting a company or have one, this book will, I hope, be both an enjoyable read and also offer value by way of tools you can actively use in your life and business to create ultimate success.

If you are in a tough place, a dark place, if you're doubting yourself or the direction you're going, there is hope. I know because I've been there. I've failed, I've lost, I'm moped, but I've turned my life around and seen so many others do so too in my time. I, therefore, know you can and will.

Thank you for picking up this book. I hope you devote yourself to the mission of reading it and using what value it offers to enrich your life and others.

I'VE BEEN THERE BEFORE.

There are a million different problems when it comes to starting and running a business. Sales and generating business are amongst one of the toughest. The number of companies that fail in their first year is scary. Most businesses fail because they couldn't sell enough of whatever it is they were trying to sell.

You'd like to think that 'fate favors the bold,' but multiple online resources suggest that 90% of businesses fail, that's 9 out of 10. Over a quarter, 1 in 4 will fail in the first year, a following 30% the following year, 50% in the fifth year. It goes on, with a lucky few making it past the big double digits, 10 years established. They are depressing numbers, but numbers we really need to use to drive us forward.

If you are an entrepreneur launching a new business, then your right to be worried. It's a big scary, nasty world out there, and at the very top, its dog eat dog. There isn't room for major error. You can have the best product or service ever invented, but if you can't sell it, then it's worthless. Creating an audience, building, or finding a market is vital.

In June 2019, I was called by a bright start-up tech entrepreneur. For the sake of privacy, I'll refer to him as John.

I went on to find out as I grew to know John that he was a gentleman in his late 30s. He was a humble yet determined man with an honest yet inspiring goal, simply to make his family proud. John's parents weren't wealthy, nor were they poor, just honest, hard-working people who also simply wanted the best for their only son. They had their ups and downs, their good times, and tough times. With a loving home and support, John focused on learning and excelled at school and university. Throughout his schooling and university life, John didn't really know where he wanted to go with his life. He did know that he didn't want to struggle or go without as he'd seen his parents do from time to time to give him the best. It was then that John knew he wanted to succeed in business, but at the same time, make a difference and have a good life doing so.

Fast-forward some years to the phone ringing and a nervous voice saying, "Hi, I read your article about sales, and I think you might be able to help." With his tail between his legs, John, sad in tone, explained how he'd founded a company with a new solution that would help small companies analyses their data and use artificial intelligence to support them to run their businesses. John had created a software platform for companies that used their data to predict, give suggest-ions, and ultimately help business owners make important decisions. The software could help companies to manage stock. It would identify when stock needed to be increased. The software took stats within data created in different parts of the business and help with challenges or questions that came about in the every-day running of a company. He talked me through the technology, explaining how it differed from the rest of the BI/AI tools and systems market because it was designed to be easy and for the small business market. Most solutions out there at the time were aimed at medium to corporate businesses, and here he had created an easy to use, simple setup tool for small, even start-ups to use to get an advantage in their market. He explained how he had created the solution when working for a company that often over-ordered stock and lost money in busy times because they weren't stocked enough.

"I think the best ideas come from problems, so many people create things, and there is no real need for them," I told him in reply to his introduction.

John had spent tens of thousands, both of his own money but also from investors in the business, which included family members and friends. I could tell by the crack of his voice he was in a bit of a rut and that he was at a crossroads. "It's a hot and cold feeling that makes me feel a tad sick at the pit of my stomach. There is this certainty there that drove me forward to here, but I've lost it a bit. I know this company can work, and this product can help people, but no one's interested," he revealed.

He had spent literally thousands on advertising online, assuming that it was the modern way to sell or that the solution would sell itself. Sometimes that very well is the case, and it's as simple as turning a key and switching on ads that deliver and generate sales. Often, online ads perform well for products, where visually, you see exactly what you're getting, and the buying process is simple.

The problem is, it's hard to communicate the benefits of the solution to a problem in a few words and a picture or short video clip. The problem wasn't that there wasn't a market for John's solution; it wasn't even that the branding or website were bad. In fact, they were great, but online advertising couldn't connect the dots easily. Customers didn't quite understand what the solution did or what problem it solved. This is often the case with new products or services; marketing and sales are as much about educating a prospect as trying to get them to get their wallet out.

"I've just burnt money advertising. Sure, we have had a couple of people request information and even a few conversations but not taken any over the line," whispered a seemingly distressed john.

John explained how he'd seen a couple of videos and read some articles I had written, and he knew that if I couldn't help him, he probably couldn't be helped. It seemed like John had gone from 100% confident in his vision to 100% with his last chips on the table. Which is what led him to me. Usually, people come to me before this point because they want my company to run a telemarketing campaign, or they want support in how to market their product or service as effectively as possible. John had tried simply advertising as a route and then felt he needed to take some steps back when it didn't work and rethink his next move. Often this happens, people make mistakes in business, and they have no option to turn around and jump in or stop and admit failure. It's easy to be scared into decisions if we are overcome by our inbuilt fear response. As an entrepreneur, you have to listen to your gut, and John did. I could tell John's heart was in his mouth, given that he was asking for my support.

"Your solution is great. I can see how it applies to businesses and how it can help them. Even your branding and website are good," I assured him.

"Why can't we close any customers? Is the price too high?" he replied, somewhat taken back by my positive words.

"What you have done is fall into the trap that a lot of entrepreneurs do. Many companies do, and it's trying to take the short cut, or you have underestimated the full sales process."

John took a deep breath in and fell silent, willing me to go on. "John, we help companies like you to thrive, to grow their businesses by generating sales opportuni-tyies with our 'done for you' lead generat-ion services as well as setting up sales funnels and sales processes. I'm sure we can turn things around for you, though I'm concerned, you've spent so much already with your advertising. I'll be honest we can help, but we're expensive."

The line fell silent for what felt like an eternity. The type of silence that sounded like a man letting go of the wheel and conceding to the crossroads of reality. It was in the moment that I thought of how low I'd been many years back, a decade before when I had to make tough decisions and changes.

Almost a decade ago, after a failed try at being a recording artist (I had a few minor successes), I was at a point in my life where I didn't know what the future held or what my next step was.

After leaving school, between jobs, I would head into London from Reading, where I grew up to spend everything I'd earnt on cutting demos and writing music. After a couple years of doing this on the weekends, I revealed to my family and friends that I was a musician and let them hear my music. I remember all the many years ago, being so scared for that moment, playing them my tracks for the first time, but they supported and stood behind me.

After negotiating a distribution deal through an arm of a major label, filming a couple of videos, travelling across the UK doing gigs and relying on promoters to plug my music, it dawned on me that it wasn't viable. Everything was costing money, and the sales didn't support it. I had some incredible fans who supported me and longed for me to find success, but it didn't pay for itself. Back then, the boom of music sharing networks, piracy, and making money from streaming and YouTube, like today, wasn't really in fruition. There are few businesses quite like the music industry, it's a tight-knit world and money, and flavor plays in. If you're not the flavor of the month or in the pockets of the people that create the playlist, then you have no hope. While I so wanted the glamours life-changing world, one pop hit at a time simply wasn't to be. I was proud of the music I made and the music I wrote with others. While there was some cheesiness, there was, I believe anyway, some heartful songs that meant more than that. I'll always be proud of what I did, even if sometimes looking back makes me cringe.

It's sad. I went through a couple of years after where I didn't want to leave my room or go out of the house. I would get to bed at 4am in the morning because I couldn't sleep and couldn't wake up until 2pm the next day. While perhaps I didn't recognize it, I was in a dark depressive place, with no one. It was like a part of me died. I would argue with my parents, who would nag me to get a job to move out, to get on with my life, but for me, I was mourning the death of who I was as an artist, what I represented and the shame I felt destroyed me. I'd told my friends and family that I would be a huge success, I'd even had small bits in the newspapers about me and my music video on a couple radios and TV shows. There is no worst feeling than to almost conquer a seemly unachievable mountain, but at the near top, when the end goal is in sight, you fall to the bottom. Not only do you lose where you are very quickly, but all the many people who stood with you in your dream for the top fall away. The people you pay to promote you, the friends who want to know you because of where you could be headed, even the women you dated disappear when your destination looks different.

After being in a rut for a couple of years, I worked myself back out into the real world and extensively learned my craft in sales. I literally went from one sales job to the next learning and earning. After years of building some sales and marketing knowledge and working my way from the bottom up, I decided to take the ultimate leap and set up my company six years ago.

I'd worked through it and got to a point where I realized no one thought about it. I knew I had to let go of what I thought others thought of me and live for me.

I decided that only I could choose to rebuild my life, and so I did step by step day by day. Today who I was and who I am now are almost two different people. If I choose to reminisce or hear a beautiful piano ballad play on the radio or in the soundtrack of a movie, for a brief moment, I connect to the sentiment, and I'm in my old shoes for a split second reliving its emotional experience.

But today I'm so removed, even tough and closed off in some ways, so different to who I was. The places, the faces, the names, the moments, the past I mourned it and spending too long there in my mind hurts.

With John, for the first time in a long time, I related to someone with this past feeling. I know the crossroads feeling all too well. Knowing that your whole world is relying on you to take something to the next level. I've felt the social pressure that we perhaps put on ourselves. While my and John stories perhaps were so very different stories, they were parallel in many ways. There was the sense of needing this to happen like there was no other option of it, conceding to fate and the reality of having to start again. I'm all for believing and inspiring others, it could be all too easy to deny that life gives us chances to protect others from the same fall, but if we don't jump and take the leap, we will never know what we can achieve. If there is one thing that entrepreneurs share, for the most part, it's that most have failed and yet that something that drives them, keeps them going until something works. Something inside me told me to offer my help, to be a good Samaritan and not ask for anything in reply, for once. A coffee, lending an ear, perhaps giving a small bit of advice or hope for what it might be worth to him. I know that if I had someone to tell me all the many years back that everything would be okay one way or another way, any way, it would have given me comfort.

"John, perhaps we can meet for a coffee and I can talk you through some ideas, and give you some advice, free of charge. If I can add some value, that way, if you see some results, then we can talk services," I suggested. I'm never like this, I've learnt to be tough, go against my soft side, but I related to his situation and what's a coffee after all.

"Thank you, that would be amazing," John said. After establishing that he was based just outside of London and that I was due to meet an editor in Mayfair from a TV production company, I suggested we meet the same day, the following Tuesday.

What I didn't know then was how this telephone call would lead to eventually changing my life, John's (who has become a great friend) life and be the catalyst of change for me. With this book, I aim to recount John's journey, showing you how I helped him turnaround his business, re-market his product and grow sales beyond his wildest imagination. It's my hope that with the tools, systems, ideas, and concepts to change your world, too, I will help you actualize your goals, launch your business, and realize your full potential. I'm not a guru or financial advisor, just a passionate entrepreneur with my own story. Ups and down and successes. I hope you enjoy both Johns story, the patches of mine, and the lessons and wisdom I've learnt and will retell in my own personal way.

I know what it's like to start with nothing and work your way up the ladder. No hand-outs, just hard work. While some label me an expert in this or a leader in that, I never used to be, I started as a young man lost without direction, holding on to a past dream but realizing that I had to change. Wherever you are in your life and your journey, whether your young and wanting to find direction or guidance to start a business or get selling, or whether you have an established business but want to sell more and sell better, this is the book for you. Read this book and apply some of the ideas that I've spent my life thus far discovering, and they will propel you forward and give you the drive and clarity to create ultimate success.

WHO ARE THEY?

*I*t's 8.15am, I realize as I look at my new diamond Rolex, which I'm now growing somewhat bored of. When I was younger, I was obsessed with the thought of having a super expensive watch. Rolex was always the one. I thought it would show the world I'd arrived. But now, as I glimpse at it, it no longer gives me the joy I anticipated it would many years ago when I was at school with a fake one I'd bought at a market on holiday in France. It's funny how when you work hard to get the things you always wanted, your desire goes, or the objects change their meaning, or you realize material things don't define you. I guess you go two ways you either lose interest in super-expensive flashy things, or you get on what they call the 'hedonistic treadmill' constantly chasing bigger and better. It's funny how when you look at the super-wealthy billionaires of the world, most have simple things. They don't have Gucci belts, gold-wrapped Ferraris or designer clothes. It's so true in this social media-saturated world we live in, most people 'flexing' their monitory muscles with material things mostly don't have much wealth and are in debt to look rich. But hey, its fun to buy cool stuff, and yes, there's a buzz to nice new things. As I have this moment of material realization, I realize I'm running late, my train is at 8.45. I'm about twenty minutes from the train station, putting my foot on the throttle.

I made the train with a few seconds to spare. As I said down, I looked through the streamed-up window at the frost on the other side of the track, feeling warm but aware of the boring 2-hour journey ahead.

Train journeys are always an awkward introspective gap of time; I always fill thinking, as if being an introvert anyhow wasn't bad enough. Lengths of time alone are just a moment to dwell or create, depending on my mood. While my thoughts skipped through my meetings, thinking of the day ahead, I couldn't help but focus on John's situation and hear his words repeat in my mind. The conversation last week had somewhat hit me. Whether it was the moral need to help someone with their problems or because I related to their predicament, I didn't know. Still, it haunted me as I sat waiting for the journey time to pass.

"It's great. I love what you said there. We'll build something around that," charmed the TV producer smiling at me as the waitress poured me another glass of champagne. I've never been one for the taste of champagne, though I've never been one to turn it down. It always says celebration or moment, but other than that fact, I prefer a beer or glass of red. Here I am sitting with a TV producer pitching me an idea for a new business TV show. It oddly feels so relevant to the person I used to be in my distant past who would have jumped at the chance. It's ironic; back in the day, it was my then team and me as a singer chasing media opportunities. Lately, it has been them chasing me, which is humbling but bitter-sweet. I'd recently said yes to filming and appearing on a light daytime TV show for the BBC about jobs, which featured me in our offices showing the role of tele sales. But now, a few opportunities have opened up with other production companies, this meeting being one. It's strange how life works. Life can often find a way of giving you what you want but the wrong way around, God's sense of humor.

It's 4pm already, and it almost slipped my mind talking about the glitz and glamour of TV, that I have a meeting with John in 15 minutes. I make my excuses and thank the TV producer for the all too expensive drink and text John that I'm running late.

I got to the restaurant. Luckily, it wasn't too far from my previous meeting. It was a charming place with a regal interior, upmarket and obviously expensive. "Hi John, nice to meet you. Nice place," I said, smiling and shaking John's hand. "Yes, I saw from your Instagram posts that you like the odd fancy place, and your kindly meeting with me, so I thought I'd find somewhere good. I've not been here before, but a college friend swears by it; apparently, the lobster is amazing." He replied.

The waiter nodded and ushered us to a table at the back with his hand. As I took a seat once more, I thought of John's position and how perhaps he'd seen our meeting and my support and advice as the answer.

"So tell me, what got you into this? How did you get started?" I questioned him while running my finger down the menu and reading the mains.

"Well, I've always been a bit of a geek, a techie. Since day dot, computers and the internet have always been my thing. My parents always had me down in their minds as a future technology whiz, but it's not gone that way. Since university, I got a job working as IT support and, while I've had a few different roles, it has always been in the same vein. The last company I was at had various problems, and at home after work, I would code. I started to develop this platform that helps use data to analyses the business and visualize the problems. I dared to take it to the managing director and, really, after talking to my friend, he said why would I hand over my own work when it could be a business. That was really the start of things. I guess you could say I fell into this," he said as he blushed.

What John had said to me, was compelling. He explained how he'd been passionate about computers and technology, falling into a series of IT support roles but there in the mix of this, he'd stumbled across a problem within a company. John has seen how he could add efficiency and clarity and help by building a solution. This is where many great businesses start from a 'problem'. Too many people try to build something when there isn't a market or try to completely reinvent the wheel. John built custom software as a solution to a problem and to improve upon a challenge. Yes, it's a growing area, but BI (business intelligence), AI (artificial intelligence) and Data solutions are relatively in their infancy. Very few small businesses use such solutions to run their business. I was interested in knowing more.

I leant back as the waiter reached in with a bottle of San Pellegrino and nodded in acknowledgement of John's story.

"The solution works well. I think it even looks good, but we've just not been able to sell it, and that's the biggest problem." John said, his eyes dimming to the side.

The problem that John was faced with is a challenge that so many creatives and new entrepreneurs have. They have a great idea, they have the concept, even the product or service, but they don't have the route to market.

So how do you take a product or service to market? You think you have an offering that there's a market for, so who is that market? Sometimes when we think about our market, our audience, or potential prospects, it's all too easy to think of them as this un-personable collective who don't have names and faces. They are numbers that serve your business. That's totally the wrong way to see it. As insignificant as you may think your potential customer is to the wider goal you have, they are paramount to your business's life and breath. There's a famous old saying that 'business isn't personal,' but it is. Every acquisition, for the most part, has had a personal choice involved. People, your customers, buy from you, or at least they buy your products or services for a reason.

While yes, it's difficult and more so on a scale to fully understand the reasoning behind a purchase on a deeply personal level, you can segment people into groups or buying profiles. A product or a service is either of two things, a solution for a problem: something that serves a purpose, fills a gap, makes life easier or something that's a nicety, a material show of worth or something that we don't need but makes us feel good or speaks to us in some way. While these two different reasons for buying are completely different, they are still determined and acquiescent to our emotions. If we are buying something or opting to use a service to solve a problem, that problem likely resonates with us. The more important the problem, the more important the solution. If we are buying a product or a service for no other reason than we want it, again, it's driven by our emotions. It either says something about us, makes us feel a certain way, or it's a subconsciously wired buying process controlled by our evolutionary or learned behaviors. When you understand that most buying is emotionally led, you can better understand the wider picture and make it more relevant to your offering.

So who is your customer, and how do we group them buy buying profile? Let's first take the instance of offering a product or service that a prospective customer needs. Who is the customer? In John's example, if you are offering a Business intelligence solution that provides a visual overview of your business in various areas, you could probably guess. In this instance, its businesses and directly, therefore, the management. It's likely straight to the top with a small business, and it will be the owner/CEO/managing director/founder. If they are slightly bigger or more in the medium SME bracket, it might be an operations director/manager/finance director/ marketing manager or director. With each different role/position, the relevance to them personally will be different, and so will be the emotional pull towards a buy. For example, an owner would buy because the problem needs fixing, and it's ultimately their company. With a different position where the individual prospect has no shareholding in the business but is an employee, the emotional reasoning sits more in the bracket of wanting to do a good job, performed well and has acquired the solution to the problem. While this can seem less emotionally committed, big purchases can be really stressful. Usually, as an owner, a longer buying process is more likely to be decided impulsively or assertively. With a non-owner, there can be more hoops to jump through.

However, additional thoughts from going to the top with your pitch are that the pitch needs to be relevant depending on the person's buying equation.

With a product or service that is a nicety, generally, there is less stress. It's more of a luxury purchase, but none the less important and may well follow the company position buying process. If it's a personal acquisition, so you're not selling to a company then, it's all about what the product or service means to the person directly. How it makes them look, feel and what they believe it says about them. When it comes to material things like clothes and designer accessories, sometimes social psychology comes into the bubble. People often think about what others think of them. This is important to remember. In fact, this point is a good one to hold onto as we talk about influence and direct sales later on in the book.

So grouping these potential prospects, you now have a way to break them into company positions or personal positions and understand the emotional relevance. It's time to look at other factors. These other factors can be a whole list of variables, Age, gender, geographic location, sector if they are a company and many more.

Ideally, you need to build an image of who your clients are. This may mean mapping out a whole combination of different probable buying personas. Selling to one individual is different from selling to another. But by understanding this, you can best augment your sales pitch and strategy to hit home.

"Hmm..." John said both in culinary enjoyment and acknowledgement of in-depth explanation of prospects more individually and in groups. Putting down the fork with the seafood linguini wrapped around it, he said," Yes, that makes a lot of sense. By seeing who a prospect is and how they might be feeling can impact their choice to buy, or even look at our services?"

"Yes, it is so important to know who your prospective client is so you can be more relevant to them." I replied, eyeing up the gourmet burger I'd ordered that had been sat in all its juicy cheesiness, teasing me as my mouth watered while explaining my point.

A LEAP OF FAITH

The warm egg yolk orange-red sun sank into the sea as I walked down the hill's aged road. I could smell grilled seafood sizzling, hear laughter and memories being made as the warm sea breeze touched my face. I was in Gozo, a little island off Malta in the med, where I'd lived for four years previously. I reached for my phone as it started to ring in my pocket, as I nodded to the tenth person I knew this evening. Living on the tiny island for a few years had really endeared me to many of the locals. It felt like a home from home, where friendly faces were all around.

"Yes," I said as I answered my phone assertively, assuming it was one of my team calling from the office. I rarely gave my mobile number out, preferring to keep business calls routed via our reception and personal assistant.

"I thought a lot about what you said, and I think I've broken potential customers into profiles," a voice said promptly. Almost three weeks had passed. I scratched my head as I recollected the voice and recounted our meeting. It was John.

"Hi, John. That's great," I sighed, trying to hide my half-hearted enthusiasm. I was thinking of my time. It had been great meeting with John and giving some advice, but I wasn't a charity after all or a friend. While I'm all for being helpful, I'm a businessman first and have a personal life. If it doesn't pay me, it doesn't serve me.

"Pierre. I want to make you an offer," he said with an extra air of confidence. As I opened a Cisk beer and poured it into the ice-cold glass, intrigue heaved my brow as I stared blankly into the distance.

"What do you mean?" I asked, somewhat perplexed. I hadn't actually proposed a campaign or even offered my consultation services, knowing full well John didn't have a budget.

"I've spoken to my bank manager, and I've explained where I'm at with the business and the mini breakthrough I had after leaving our meeting. It's all too obvious that I've just not thought about selling or marketing in the right way. I hadn't really set money aside for sales. Only the advertising, but I've agreed to a loan to get this going right. It's not a lot, but it's something." He said with his words coming at one hundred miles an hour.

"John, we're expensive. But yes, I'm sure we can help, though it's going to take time, and we're currently at capacity with work. We actually currently have a client waiting list." I replied.

"Don't worry about a campaign. Let me sit in with you, with your team, let me learn 'how to sell.' I spoke to Rich, one of your guys, and he said you're not traditional with your teaching. You're innovative and passionate. I can tell that from your articles, videos, and our meeting. I know you don't have time but let me shadow you for ten days. One day a month for the next 10 months. I'll give you my full sales budget, £20,000." He said, waiting for my answer before he'd even got all the words out.

I paused for a moment and thought— £2,000 a day to shadow me in the office and learn like a new recruit. While campaigns can run significantly more than this, the offer seemed reasonable at the time. But most compelling to me, above all else, was that this individual was willing to take out a loan and place all of his and his company's faith in me and my sales and marketing experience. I felt a huge weight on my shoulders. I knew how important this next year would be for John in getting his business to work. It was all or nothing.

"Yes. I'm out of the country at the moment, but I'm back in a week. Come to our London office the Monday after next, and I'll introduce you to the team." I said, wondering what the next few months would bring.

Sometimes in life, to achieve great things or get through difficult times, we have to act on faith. Everything can be against you, and yet you see a path. And while it can seem obvious or even a difficult choice, you know in your heart of hearts that its where you need to go. Retrospectively now, when I think about it, I imagine how hard it must have been for

John to pick up the phone and ask me for that. He did it with such commitment, as if he knew I wouldn't say no. Deep down, as he made the choices, he must have considered as he's ticked off all his other options that there could be a chance I wouldn't welcome the offer. But he took the chance. John ultimately had faith in himself and his company. He knew if he could learn how to sell, learn how to market, that it might give him a chance of turning everything around.

As I boarded the plane, looking at my tanned swede boating shoes as they walked up the staircase, my mind wondered. I thought to myself how life is like a journey. Not just one journey, but a series of journeys, with different destinations, creating different moments in our timeline. I thought about how monumental each moment we have is and thought back to points in my life from being a boy at school to holding my own baby boy in my arms. There is a saying that travel broadens the mind. I think that is so true; firstly, it offers you a difference in culture and location. Secondly, travelling offers you contrast to see your own life externally from outside the box. I knew when I got back, I would focus on my business and driving it forward. That moment made me think about the people that relied on me—my team, my family, and now this other individual who was investing in his own success.

STANDING ON THEIR SHOULDERS

"*O*ne Large Black Americano extra shot," said the Barista as she handed me the warm cup carefully wrapped in napkins. "That will wake you up," she joked with a coy smile, something she undoubtedly says to all the half-asleep zombie Londoners that pass through needing a quick fix. "I need it," I replied as I walked out of the coffee shop, leaving the heavenly smell of roasted coffee beans behind, clutching to my now burning hot cup of morning magic. I love coffee, all caffeine, for that matter. I find it gives the perfect kick in the head to get the cogs turning. It's crazy when you realise that caffeine or trimethylxanthine, as it is better known in the neurochemistry world, is actually seen more like a drug that stimulates the central nervous system, much like other more illegal stimulants. Nevertheless, this psycho-active drug is the drug of choice for half the world, certainly most business professionals. The sales industry wouldn't be the same without it.

The lift rushes up as I see the floor numbers roll as we pass them. Finally, floor 25. Whenever I step foot into the London office, the view and the prestige hit me, and it never wears off. There's something special about working high-up amongst the clouds that gives you a sense of achievement and purpose.

"I have, John, waiting for you over there, Pierre," said Melissa, the receptionist, as she nodded to the window overlooking London Bridge station.

"It's quite something, isn't it," I said as I walked over to the window John was looking out of, "you can see St. Pauls cathedral over there." I pointed to the furthest window to the left.

"I can see why you're based here. It's amazing, very inspiring," John comment-ed.

"It's a great headquarters for the business, I'm not here much, but every time I am, it has the same effect. It reminds me of the famous saying of how we are 'standing on the shoulders of giants.' You just have to look at the architecture around us down there to see the incredible man-made accomplishments. How far we've come from carving out objects with stone tools to carving out great monuments and builds through time. It's inspiring."

John stood there for a moment, frozen in thought, as he glanced through the surrounding windows at the London skyline. "Shall we?" I prompted as I gestured to one of the many meeting rooms.

We walked over to the meeting room, where the conversation in the room silenced as we entered. "Morning guys," I said sharply to my team, all suited and booted with every bright coloured tie you could imagine. I have a policy that resonates with many sales offices, and I believe it is true; if you dress the part, you'll act the part. It plays into the psychology of sales.

"I'd like to introduce you to John. He's a client of ours, here today to experience being in the team and to learn how to sell first-hand." I revealed to the inquisitive eyes of my team.

"Lesson number one dress to impress. Even though we're on the phone, we need to feel on top of the world. Sales is like method acting; you have to truly embody that which you want to shine out. Confidence comes with smartness. "What's with your shoes, Matt?" I pointed to his scruffy pair of loafers. "Sorry, the heel came off my new shoes, and I've not had the chance to go get some more or get them repaired, so I wore an old pair." "How are you supposed to close high-flyers when you look like you're wearing your dads clapped out old shoes he found in a skip?" I said with bravado. "Go, buy some new shoes now and bring me the receipt. If you close a deal this afternoon, I'll buy them. If you don't, they'll be out of your commission this month."

Matt nodded and headed for the door. The rest of the team nervously adjusted their ties, clicked their pens, and readied themselves. I stood back and whispered to John, "that's how you keep a team sharp and on edge. If you find a weakness, you call them on it. Outline expectations and discipline them. It will define the best from the rest. You're not in business to carry dead weight. Yes, people are people, and you reward them as such, but you have to keep the dividing lines very clear. They need to know their boss is not their friend, and if they don't like it or can't perform, you replace them. Conversely, if people perform well, treat them like knights. Well rewarded for their honour in a successful battle, but never too complacent.

If there is one thing I have learnt, and I've learnt the tough way, it's that being soft doesn't get you anywhere. I crafted my management style to have a clear separation between work life and personal life. People will take advantage of your good nature if you treat them like a friend. If you want lazy, unrespectful or unmotivated staff, be their mate. If you want hard-working individuals, let them earn your respect.

Of course, there are many different management styles, and there are other styles that individually manage and motivate. But as a stereotypical route, this tough leader style works best in sales.

"Today, we're going to go through everything from start to finish. I know you've all be through this with me several times. But as you know, revising the process and re-evaluating ourselves with methods and strategies has a great outcome and helps keep us focused. Also, we have John here, as I mentioned, and I want to give him a transparent look at what we do, how we sell, and some of the tool and tips we have to create better results." I announced.

I walked over to the middle of the meeting room and switched on the projector, which beamed onto the white canvas, "How to sell on the phone."

SELLING ON THE PHONE

INTRODUCTION/OBJECTIVE – CREATING AN OUTCOME

*I*t's super important that you truly are ready when it comes to preparing for a sales call. But what does that mean? Firstly, you need to make sure that your heads screwed on and that you're in a positive mind frame. It's all too easy to let personal matters or stress get in the way, and so it's important to leave everything at the office door when you enter to get deals done. The way you hold yourself, sit and hold your phone all have an impact. If you are slumped at your desk acting like an idiot, you'll most probably perform like one. Having the correct physical and mental form is key to being on point and sharp. The physical does alter the mental. I 100% believe that. You can take being in the correct mental zone to the extreme, with the rituals you have, the way you dress, even down to the cologne you wear. If it makes you feel good, then you're halfway there.

When you're looking and feeling on form, the next step is to make sure you are prepared with all the materials you need. Your data, the prospects, list of names and contact details for calls, and your sales pitch that you'll use not as a read announcement but as a guide.

Now you have everything to hand and are sitting there poised to get calling; you need to think objectively. What is it? It's easy when you're selling on the phone to assume you just start talking to the prospect and expect results to happen. You need to have a clear route to a result; you need to know what you want, whether that is an email, looking to generate a lead or an appointment or whether you want to close a deal. Hopefully, if you are a budding salesperson, you've watched all the great movies that depict high-flying sales-people. Like them, you need to get into character. Be super confident, super sharp, a listening ear but with a definitive result in mind. Many salespeople working with me nervously ask, "How can I be more confident?" The simple answer I often give them is 'fake it' – put on an act, hide behind the sales persona. It makes it easier. You will soon find after a couple of dozen calls, it won't feel so scary.

After that, when the pitch sounds natural, your pitch will automatically sound and seem more confident. There are many techniques I like to use with my team, but one gem I use to help newbies get over the intimidation of calling is to give them a storyline. I tell them that they are a marine hiding out in the woods, its dark, late at night with the visual target in view. The target is walking around in his warm, light, house, open and visual to the select few marines sighting him up with their snipers. Obviously, the target, a super bad criminal, terrorist, or warlord, is completely unaware of the preparation going into their takeout. There's plenty of distance between you and your target and you're concealed in the woods with a team around you. Undoubtedly, if you didn't have some adrenaline, you wouldn't be human, but when you can rid yourself of negative emotions and realise that you are in complete control, you don't fear the target, just like making a call. They don't know who you are, they don't know the preparation and work that has gone into the words you're going to say, and you are in control. If you've got good data and done a little research on a prospect, you know who they are. They have no clue who you are. If you make a mistake, miss your shot, you can retreat, and you have the team around you for support. But the good news in sales is that unless you are selling a product or service with a limited potential audience, you have ·lots of prospects, so not getting every target isn't a problem, move on to the next.

By thinking like this and finding ways to relate takes away fear and stress. Ultimately, don't stress. You can always apologise and say you are new if you don't have the answers when questioned on a pitch (hopefully you do) and suggest getting back to them.

GATEKEEPER / GETTING THROUGH TO THE DECISION-MAKER

'Gatekeepers,' an industry term for the receptionists or people that answer the phone who route the call to a decision-maker or more often take a message or make an excuse. This is another common area newbies bring up. Their hate of 'being shut down,' 'closed off' or 'told no' by a gatekeeper.

Let's get one thing straight, it's their job! As soon as you realise that, and know it's not personal, you are over step one of multiple step hurdles, which is getting to the decision-maker. Psychologically, for a moment, put yourself into the shoes of the gatekeeper and try and hear their tone of voice. You can often work out a lot about someone by the way they talk, pitch, speed, accent, age, confidence level and so on. By segmenting them into a profile in your mind, you can work out what strategy to take with each, and there are many. I tend to initially teach two direct approaches. The two approaches couldn't be more different from each other, but if you can learn when to use them in accordance with your gatekeeper, you will have the best chance of getting through or getting vital intelligence.

Number one is authoritative, sharp, to the point/matter of fact, and demanding. – This approach is where you take the stance of you being important and them being a receptionist. As condescending as it sounds, it plays on social psychology. If they think you're important, and that's reflected in your tone, they will first ask fewer questions, and secondly, they will be more adhering to your request. This works well with younger, less long-in-the-tooth gatekeepers, with less experience of seeing through the veneer of a self-confident salesperson. If you watch TV and movie representation of confident people or authority with socially higher-standing, they almost come across as rude. For example, 'put me through to John Smith, please. Tell him its Joe Bloggs.' This approach, because it is borderline dictatorial, is so confident that you wouldn't want to disagree. However, if you get the wrong type of gatekeeper, a more experienced one or one that loves confrontation (you do get them), they will jump in with a counter authority question. In this instance, you can either jump straight to approach two, which I'll cover in a second, or you can answer with any of the following, if you're feeling daring and if it's appropriate; 1. 'He's expecting my call' – when you get through you explain they may be aware of you as you believe they would have had an email from you. 2. 'Sorry what's your name and position? Can you make business decisions, no? Then can you put me through? – this is abrupt and only used in the scenario that you think they are bluffing at being tough, and a second push would get you through. 3. Lastly, sure, no worries I'll drop him an email.

The second approach is super polite, nice, inoffensive, softly spoken but with an inquisitive consultative edge. Sometimes by being really nice and friendly and asking or pleading, you can build a rapport with a gatekeeper, who may put you through or give you some valuable information. This works well when a gatekeeper is seemingly happy, something you can tell from their pitch and way of speaking.

It is good to note that if you do call back in a couple of days and speak to the same gatekeeper, they likely won't remember you. So you can use the counter approach and see if this gives you more results.

My presentation concluded with me asking if there were any questions on the slide. I paused and pulled out my iPhone. "Matt, where are you? You've been almost two hours?" I quizzed.

"I'm literally two mins from the foyer now," he replied, short of breath, as though he'd run back in a hurry.

"Okay, meet us down in the foyer in five mins," I ordered. "Right, everyone, shall we put Matt to the test?" I laughed. "Let's see if he can pitch. Let's go downstairs and see these shoes!"

Sitting on the foyer reception chair was a flushed Matt, grinning at his new shoes.

"Very nice. I didn't think there was a Mothercare around here?" I joked, looking at the small new shoes on his feet, as the team laughed. "Right follow me guys." The team, John in tow, looked perplexed as I guided them back to the lift we'd just exited.

"What do salespeople call our sales pitch?" I asked the team.

"Lift speech," said a few.

"Elevator pitch," said Matt, guessing what was about to happen.

"You got it!" I smiled, "The reason us salespeople call it that is you should be able to pitch something in thirty seconds or a short lift-ride up. We're on the 25th floor. Let's see how you do, Matt. Pitch to John on those new shoes, let's go."

Matt took a deep breath in, and we all stepped into the lift. "Ring Ring. Hi, its Matt from Feel Good Feet. Can I speak to John?" he opened.

"Yes, speaking," John replied.

"John, I call people like you every day who commute and work long days in the office, and a problem they find is that they get sore feet and can't wait to take their shoes off at the end of the day. Can you relate?"

"Yes," John replied, taken back and seemingly impressed by Matt's pitch. "You know I do."

"Well, John, the good news is we have Feel Good shoes that don't just solve that problem, they feel great. And best of all, are more affordable and harder wearing than other leading shoes. Can I send you a catalogue?"

"Absolutely." John agreed.

"Ah you were too soft on him," I directed at John as the team sniggered behind me. "That was good. See what Matt did, quickly got to the point, explained what he was selling, created a problem and made John agree it was a potential solution and would save him money, double whammy! Oh, and here we are our floor." I said as the lift doors opened.

We walked through the office and over to the kitchen, where I gestured to the team to grab a coffee or refreshment before heading back into the meeting room.

"Perfect, this takes me on to the next slide," I grinned as the team returned to their seats.

ASKING QUESTIONS

"This is what Matt did when he aligned a problem in the pitch for John, but let's looks at the way we can ask more questions and look at why asking questions is so important."

Asking questions is one true way to engage a prospective buyer. Firstly, you can see if they have been listening and are invested enough to respond, but mostly it gives you valuable 'intelligence' to work with. When you try to make a case or pitch a product or service, you have to frame it in a way to make the prospect see it as relevant. By asking questions that yield the answers you want or giving you the direction to lead the prospect along, helps you move the pitch to a close.

One of the biggest misconceptions is that all salespeople are good at is talking. They should be good at it, but a salesperson, perhaps, most important skill set is their ability to listen and ask questions. People like to talk. It's a fact. Sales newbies often ask me, 'how do you build rapport?' One of the quickest ways is to listen, ask questions, and seem interested. People will often tell you their life stories, which often allows you to use fact-building to strengthen your proposition.

So what are the types of question you should be asking to get the maximum information from a prospect? Here are a few examples:

Is this something you have used/looked at before? – This is to get them to tell you whether or not they have used a similar product or service before or if they have considered it.

Do you find (enter sector problem or challenge)? – This will get them to tell you whether or not they align with some of the pain points you've drawn on in your problem/solution type pitch. Like Matt asked John, "Do you relate?" when he mentioned sore feet, long commutes and walking lots in his elevator pitch.

Do you have a timeline where you may be looking at this? – If the prospect sides with your suggestions and agrees that they are or have indeed looked at this offering, it is key that you try to understand what their timeline is and when they might look to start their looking process.

If it's more straight forward or a less price-conscious buy then you might ask them, 'What would you look for in (insert product or services)?' – This question will open them up to explain what they need and are looking for, and this will help you to best frame your offering for what they require, morally, of course.

There are many other questions you can use here that will be more specific to what you are looking to sell. The more experience you acquire, the better you will become at asking the right questions.

Remember, asking the right questions not only gives you the information to understand their situation, but it also allows you to best pitch or frame your offer to make it as relative as possible.

OBJECTION HANDLING

This has to be the area I see most people fail, certainly newbies and not great salespeople. The client offers an objection, and they close you down. Sometimes a prospect will offer an objection by way of finding out more or to negotiate or take back some of the power in the conversation. It's important to work out what's behind the objection. If an objection is direct, and the objection is specific, for example, price or product-specific, then deal with the objection head-on.

How do you deal with an objection? While there are a few ways, one of the best is to agree. By acknowledging their objection, 'I understand what you're saying. It is expensive, however....' By first recognizing their key problem you can explain why perhaps they are not correct. For example, you could go on to say... 'however, the price is slightly higher because the product lasts three times longer than regular counterparts. Significantly saving you money in the long run.' It's not always going to be possible to overcome every objection. If they keep objecting for different reasons then perhaps, they aren't in the market for your offer. There is a general misconception that a good salesperson can sell anything to anyone. Certainly, there's some truth to that, but ultimately, if someone isn't in the market for your product or service, then you may well be more productive just moving on. Sales is ultimately a numbers game, after all.

One of the best things to do, and I highly recommend it to help you overcome objections, is to create an objection handling document. What is it? It's a spreadsheet or list of common objections and pre-rehearsed comeback answers. Remember to factor in acknowledging their objections. If you keep coming back to the prospect with answer after answer but don't acknowledge an objection or two, they will most likely get annoyed or feel inferior to your smart and quick over prepared sales style. It's important, like any negotiation, to give and take or give that impression. Ultimately, you want to dominate, but sometimes you have to play a game of cat and mouse.

CLOSING

How do you close? The million-dollar question or more if you're closing a bigger deal. You ask for it! Most the time, it's that simple, and yet, people are just too scared to do it. There are many ways to skin a rabbit, as they say, but when it comes to closing, it's about asking what's next. Asking if they want you to send a booking form, an invoice. It's asking for the next step. If you're closing for the next step of a sale process with a longer lead product or service, it may mean closing with a set appointment date or asking for their email to send them the order form. Closing is half dependent on your sales process and onboarding, but also on their timeline, which by now you should know. The best way to close is to take the intelligence you've gathered in the call and factor in their timeline accountably. Make them take action, whether it is agreeing on an appointment date or getting them to agree to send back your order form.

If it's a shorter sell or a lower price buy, then you can use the offer and create urgency by expressing how time limited or availability restricted the offering is. If you do a good job of relating the product or service to the prospect, closing will be easier.

PUTTING A TELESALES SCRIPT TOGETHER

Let's look at a script. Firstly, let me just say for the record, I don't believe in scripts for reading a pitch. To me, they are more of a guide. Everyone, I'm sure, has been contacted at some point by a phone company trying to sell you an upgrade or new contract with the tendency to sound robotic and 'salesy,' lacking personality, and you can tell the marketers are new to sales. It's important to have a structure for a sale pitch, and by creating a script, you can map it out, including the questions you want to ask. By creating a script and laying it out in points, you can easily bring yourself back to the topic if you feel yourself going off subject or not heading toward the close you want.

Unless you are selling something really technical or specialist, most scripts will take a similar direction to this. Below is my 'Insert the X Sales Pitch' which can be altered to sell anything. Of course, if you are going to create a top-notch script you will need to flesh it out a bit. This is the bare bones, and you must enrich it.

Basic Script Guide

Gatekeeper Stage:

'Good morning/Good afternoon, Can I speak to (Insert DM Name)' – The aim really when trying to get through is not to give away too much information. The reason is, it will allow a gatekeeper to shut you down, and they may remember, so when you try calling back they will close you down.

In the scenario that the gatekeeper asked the reason for the call, there are multiple responses. Here are a few good key options:

'It's with regards to (insert problem/job role/product or service)'

'He/She should be aware of my call' (This is a little fib/mistruth, but can easily be brushed under the carpet, when transferred to the prospect, by saying, 'I believe you may be aware of me calling as, I tried to call last week/I sent you an email a couple days ago).

'I've been asked to give him a call back by my colleague, it's with regards to (insert problem/job role/product or service).' This is a bit of a white lie, but one you can pass off by saying, 'I thought they may have called you, I apologies, the reason for the call is...'

'It's a personal/confidential call' – (a great way to get through, but only to be used where it's a product or service that may be relevant to them directly or an aspect of the business-like finance. Something that wouldn't be openly discussed with all the staff members).

The truth is there are lots of ways to get through the gatekeeper. The more imaginary, the better, though it's important to keep in mind that telling white lies are very borderline and only to be used with confidence. It's also important to verify with your manager or boss that they are happy for you to tell white lies to get through. They are only white lies; most salespeople use them to get through initially.

On to the main decision-maker pitch script. This is really, as I mentioned before, the bare bones. But a key structure for most B2B (Business to Business) sales pitches, B2C (Business to consumer), are different but with similarities. Think between the lines and decide how you would adapt it.

Hi (Insert DM prospect name),

It's (*insert your name*) from (*insert company name*). Thank you for taking my call. I appreciate your time. I'll keep it brief (The thanking part is an optional line but is beneficial as thanking them for their time means they are less likely to close you down based on time. It's a tad passive-aggressive but can work well)

(*insert prospect first name* – You can start with their name; this will make them listen. It's a trick wired into us from a young age. Our name makes us listen. Its super important, however, that you don't overuse it. I would suggest only using it in an open and possibly, if it feels right, in a close. **The reason for the call today is, we work with companies like yours in the (*insert sector*) sector, for example (*competitor insert name drop* –** These are the names of other customers you have. The more relevant to them, the better, if you don't have any, skip the name drop and just say the sector**, and we (*insert your added value* –** this maybe 'help them save money on' or 'we help them find good candidates' or 'we provide them with low-cost, high-quality coffee beans.' You need to find which angle best defines the value your offering adds and express it to them.

(*Insert product or service features and benefits*, perhaps with a brief anecdote that relates and builds rapport, so long as its relevant and doesn't sound canned. In these few lines, you want to add some color to the picture, some relevance – For example, 'our coffee beans are fair trade and sourced directly from the producer, this means not only are we making a difference locally in the communities that are better rewarded, but because we cut out the middlemen companies, we can provide coffee to you at a more cost-effective price.')

May I ask... (insert opening question) that gets them talking to you – for example, 'How often do you buy coffee beans for the office?' or 'What do you tend to do when you're looking for a new member of staff?' The key here is to ask questions that give you something to work with or to help understand their situation in view to needing your offering. What's super important is that you don't ask yes or no questions. What I mean by that is if you ask, 'are you employing new staff right now?' They could simply say, 'no.' Sometimes people don't like sales calls, they will naturally try to close you down and asking 'yes' or 'no' questions will give them the perfect opportunity to close off the conversation. They will also often say 'no' even if the answer is yes because they don't want to talk to you. If, however, you ask them questions that get them talking and they start telling you more, they will feel more comfortable, and you can lead the direction.)

Let the prospect speak and listen

(Insert secondary rely on question – 'so when you buy coffee from the supermarket, how much do you intend to spend?' or 'How much time do you tend to spend going to the shops each week or month for the coffee?' – The secondary questions need to open up some pain, (when I say pain, this is the sales term for finding the most relative emotion and pulling on it) or more information to help you find a close.)

Let the prospect speak and listen

(Insert your custom close – This will be based very much on your product or service and the corresponding sales process you have in place. With simple buys, you can go for the close immedia-tely. But, if it's a higher value product or service, there may be additional steps. This is the case a lot of the time. Therefore, your close needs to be asking for either the sale, the follow up action (call back schedule), a meeting booked in (face to face or over the phone/online) or their email for more information. Unfortunately, while you can create urgency and use offers and other tools, a prospect will often have a timeline for acquiring a product or service, more so when it is of high value. This initial cold call would act as a first sales touchpoint. You may need a few to get them to buy. Here is an example of the different closes:

Sales – 'We currently have a special on three units of coffee beans, which comes in at just under what you're spending at the supermarket and it saves you time as well. Would you like to place an order?'

Follow up. 'As you mentioned, you may be looking to bring a new team member on board at the end of next month. Shall I give you a call back on (insert suggested call date).'

Booking a Sales meeting – 'It would be great to tell you more about our recruitment services and find out more about your company to see how we can align our services to support you. Is there a good time next week? 'Tuesday or Thursday' Giving two different options is called the tea or coffee close. I mentioned it on the BBC One show, Call That Hard Work. This is a simple technique with the desired effect of having the prospect pick one of the two suggested options.'

Email request – 'Okay, great. Well perhaps I can send some more informat-ion over to you, so you can see our range/find out more about our services. What the best email for you?'

That is the bare bones of a cold call sales script. Of course, this is one example, there are others. But this is one you can use, adapt, and tweak to give you the relevant structure to open and close. I've not mentioned the objection handling there, but as I mentioned earlier, if you make a list or document all the top possible objections and build good answers, you can deal with them as and when they come in to play throughout the call, and they likely will.

If you do get taken off subject or get lost in answering an objection, bring yourself back to the script as a guide in front of you, work out whereabouts you are in the pitch and get back on track.

If you use these techniques, tips, and material to master 'cold calling,' you will sail to sales when it comes to pitching a prospect that has already enquired or who has submitted their information online. When you have a sales strategy that focuses on creating warm leads to call, you will strap a rocket on your feet, and you can shoot for the stars when it comes to sales. We will look at how to create warm leads in the next chapter.

"Ahh, lovely, there's nothing like a good old pint of beer to close a long day in the office," Matt said, taking a look at his honey-orange refreshing liquid in his cold pint glass.

"Oh yes," replied John, taking a sip.

"I don't know if it's a sales thing or a London thing, but the afternoon pitching doesn't half feel better knowing there's a nice pint waiting after," said Jake, another member of the team, as we all smiled and laughed in agreement.

"Today was insightful. Lots to take in, but I feel I've got a good idea of how to pick up the phone and pitch now." John said as he looked at me.

"Yes, you know your prospects, and now you have a structure to pitch with that you can adapt and make relevant to each different type of prospect," I said, agreeing with him. "Now you have the pitch down, next is the overall sales process. We'll define your sales strategy and where that pitch fits in, but that's for another day. I'm not sure what day you want to put in the diary for next month, but I'm away on business in Ireland, fancy a Guinness?"

SWEET MUSIC ON THE HARP OF DUBLIN

*L*adies and Gentlemen, welcome to Dublin, Ireland. The local time is 8am," said the captain as we landed on the runway. The rain was pouring down the window as we looked out at a slightly grey but fresh-looking day.

We quickly passed through passport control and were in the taxi heading into the city. "I don't know about you, but I'm thinking a spot of breakfast wouldn't go amiss. Even though it's probably more lunchtime on my bodies time clock," I said, thinking of the ghastly hour I woke up to head to the airport. Even though the flight time was a mere hour and a half, security and all that meant I was up at 5am, leaving the hotel. My stomach was making knotted turns at the delighting thought of tongue tantalising bacon, sausages, white & black pudding, and toast with Irish butter.

"This is a breakfast and a half," John said as he pushed some baked beans on to the piece of sausage on the end of his fork.

"Can you beat a meaty breakfast? English, Irish, Scottish, American. Nothing beats eggs and bacon in the morning," I said, agreeing with John, as I raised the glass of water to cleanse my pallet.

We watched the traffic go by in the street as we waited for the waitress to bring the check. "It's weird. There are almost two schools of thought when it comes to breakfast. Some say you should 'Eat like a king in the morning to prepare yourself for the day,' and then there's the new breed of intermittent fasters. Have you heard of that?" I questioned John, reaching in my pocket for my credit card.

I've become really fascinated in the area of Biohacking after reading a book called 'Superhuman' by Dave Asprey, a bestselling author and 'The father of Biohacking.' It's about taking your health into your own hands and implementing changes creating longevity while also feeling better. The book introduced me to the concept of fasting, which I've explored since. The book and other articles and knowledge out there point to the fact that as humans, we simply aren't made to eat all the time. As we've advanced in technology and food production, it's all too easy to overeat, leading to health problems. By fasting either intermittently or for longer periods, it's thought to start the body's natural Autophagy mechanism, which allows the body to use and consume bad cells. Intermittent fasting is also suggested to release growth hormone into the body, which keeps us young. New research by Dr Jason Fung in his book 'The Diabetes Code' suggests that type II Diabetes with fasting can be reversed.

John looked at me with half a mouth full of toast, "Yes, I've heard about it, but I'm too into my food."

"Yeah, it's tough. I know the health benefits are massive, but it's a struggle when you're a foodie, right?" I added as we laughed.

I try to do 2–3-day fasts once a month or two from time to time. Not only does it have health benefits, but it also builds mental toughness (it's not easy).

"So this afternoon, I'm talking at a Small Business Marketing event on how to create the perfect sales strategy. It couldn't be any more perfect timing-wise, right?" I said to John as he nodded in agreement.

I often like to accept speaking engagements. Not only does it feel good to give back and inspire others, but it keeps you at the forefront of people's minds, supporting you in being a thought leader in your field.

After an hour or two walking around the shops and a quick pop into the Dublin office (Big Wolf Marketing; my agency has a small setup in Ireland), we headed to the event venue.

The venue was an old church hall with seating all pointed towards the stage. I often wish I knew more about architect-ure and the history of building periods to correctly describe it. But it was a beautiful building, no doubt steeped in history and meaning. Buildings like this often make me feel humbled by the power and greatness of the generations before us. Beacons of art, they stand through time, representing a vision of prestige and power.

As we walked up to the front of the stage, the event manager came over to me. "One of our speakers isn't well today, so it's just you and another speaker. Could you fill the time of two talks?" he said, seeming somewhat stressed out.

"Yes, of course, I might waffle, but I do that anyway. But yes, there's lots to get through, so I'd be happy to,' I replied, internally wondering what to do but reassuring myself that I tend to talk over my time anyway.

"Please welcome to the stage, Sales and Marketing expert, Entrepreneur and Big Wolf Marketing Founder, Pierre Coombes," the events manager announced into the microphone as the growing swell of people applauded across the seating.

"Thank you very much. It's great to be back in Dublin." I said, taking the microphone, looking out over the audience.

"The reason you're all here today is likely because your passionate about business, your business, and you don't just want to succeed; you want to thrive. You can. It doesn't matter what you sell, within reason, so long as you can find a route to market. But, and but is the keyword, how do we know the best way to sell? There are so many different ways to sell these days. Everyone says it's a different channel, a different communication medium, and everyone will have their own preference. I'm going to tell you, but you might not like the answer. It's 'everything,' using them all! Buying and being sold to these days is a new experience; our decisions are being made by various influencing 'touches' as we call them in marketing. What does that mean in non-jargon? Well, we need to see the offering in multiple places or have multiple contact points with the brand or company.

These days when we want to buy something, we research it, we watch countless YouTube videos on that item, right? The internet has changed the way we buy for sure, and you might think that's bad news to a sales expert whose main field of expertise is phone sales. But no, its great news. Never before have we been at such a point where we can build warm interest before even making contact. Twenty plus years ago, you had to cold call people to get results and work on them, build pipeline and take time converting them. For sure, it still works, but with online lead generation and telemarketing combined, it's powerful! In the past, the best warm leads you had were the very few people that might call in having seen an advert and trust me, they were like gold; they still are. These days you can literally automatize lead generation online. When you do, the warm data of prospects will give you the best conversion." I started to explain to the audience.

When you are looking to sell long term, you really need a strategy that yields constancy that will give you a measurable return on investment. What you need is a sales funnel! Your client journey, how you find a prospect and how you engage with them, to ultimately how you close them.

There are two key ways as a starting point to creating interest in your product or service. One is slower than the other, but they both have their pros and cons.

CONTENT MARKETING –

This is, as it would suggest, where you create engaging content, articles, blogs, infographics, videos and searching and sharing the content via social media. Traffic interested in your content will engage with it. As long as you have an opt-in email form, visible contract details or a more detailed lead form, visitors can request more information. Some of the best content marketing tips are to offer information, eBooks, whitepapers, case studies and pricing lists as a download or requestable asset. Securing contact details is securing interest. It's unlikely that a prospect visiting will request information or engage if they aren't in the market for a product or service like yours. There are also a couple of analytic tools out there online that will give you details of who has visited your site. The benefit, of course, is because not all the traffic that clicks through to your website is going to submit their information. These tools can be a little grey as they often can tell you the company that has visited your website, but not the exact individual. This can be overcome by searching LinkedIn for employees and finding the most likely fitting individual. This isn't a perfect art but can work, sometimes it's worth noting down multiple individuals you believe could be the decision-makers relating to your offer. There is a great tool at www.hunter.io that lets you search a company URL and find the team's email addresses. If you have a name, you can often search for direct emails, which is a great way to reach out. When you start to collect both the submitted inquiries and the visitor insight prospect profiles, you build a warm database of leads to call in the next phase of your sales funnel.

The second more popular, quicker, easier, and more expensive route is advertising on Google, Facebook, LinkedIn, and other major social media site/platforms. However, the key with these, like with building natural traffic with content creation, is that you also make sure to capture visitors' details with forms and email lists and make your contact details prominent. The best bit about many of these adverting tools now on the major platform on Facebook is the option to create a lead capture form built into the ad, so a prospect can submit their details straight away, without losing them in the click through to your website. This lead generating shortcut is the best development in online advertising. If you use it, you are creating a list of warm leads without having to pay to simply send them to your website to hope they submit a form because most visitors won't –the more engaging the ads, the better the conversion. We will look at ad copy in the next chapter.

Now you have the starting point for your sales funnel. The first stage is finding interested prospects. The second part, equally as important, is engaging with those prospects. The great news is that you are now knowledgeable about making a cold call from reading the previous chapter. Making a call to reach out to a warm prospect, one that reached out to you by either visiting your website or, even better, submitting their details to you, should make cold calling much easier!

Here's a simple example. Again, a bare-bones mini script of the type of conversation you would have when reaching out to a warm prospect.

"Hi **(insert prospect name)**, it's **(insert your name)** from **(insert company).** Thank you for responding to our ad on Facebook. I saw that you submitted your details and thought I'd reach out to see how we may be able to help. **(Insert question to secure more information** – for example, 'What type of coffee do you purchase at the moment?' or 'What do you currently do when you're looking to bring a new team member onboard?').

If they haven't submitted their details, but you have used the tools to see the companies visiting your website and have researched their name and contact details and are looking to call them, you might wish to use this instead:

"Hi **(insert prospect name)**, it's **(insert your name)** from **(insert company)**. We have a clever tool on our website that looks at companies that have visited, and I've noticed **(insert company name).** I did a bit of research and thought it might be you? **(Insert question to secure more information** – for example, 'What type of coffee do you purchase at the moment?' or 'What do you currently do when you're looking to bring a new team member onboard?')

When you have done a warm lead reach out, you may have some leads that are actionably keen to close or have more information. If not, you want to make sure they are in your CRM (Customer Relationship Manager – a solution or program that clients details are sorted in) or spreadsheet for calling back or email follow-up.

It's very easy to let leads go cold. If you speak to a prospect that's not interested yet, or needs follow up or is a longer lead, you need to make sure you are actively marketing to them. This leads to the third step, optional but strong in creating results; email marketing/email automation.

Letting prospects go cold just isn't a good move. Using email marketing or, better, email automation, you can drip feed your warm prospects information, offers, and invites via creating emails. They shouldn't always be sales focused but should offer the prospect value. For example, you might have one email as a case study and another as sector stats. This will keep them engaged and have you in their mind as a leader in your area.

This three-pronged approach to finding, engaging, nurturing, and closing creates real and definitive results. Combining multiple marketing methods creates a snowball effect with a client as you build rapport at each point of engagement.

After I'd explained the concept of a sales funnel and how companies need to really think about their sales strategy, I put down the presentation clicker.

"You see, sales don't always need to be so direct. If you offer value by way of information or convey an idea, product or service in the right way, be it with an offer, a whitepaper, something that hooks a lead, you don't need to be so cold in your sales approach. With the right strategy, a prospect is ready to be sold to. By no way am I saying telesales or cold telemarketing is dead. I can't. I'm a telesales man by trade, but with digital engagement as a cultivator of interest, you can use the phone to its biggest potential. "Strategy is everything!" I said as I closed, the room applauded. I blushed and nodded, humbled by the reaction.

There's nothing quite like the feeling you might just have inspired a few to go on and make changes that will help them create real tangible results.

"Hey man, that was great! Really good and powerful. I'm piecing it together now, how a strategy works or a funnel, as you said. It's not just black or white, telesales or running ads. It's the merge of the different methods done together as a mutual effort. I see that now. I don't know why, but when you think of sales and marketing, you also see them as two different things. They are so interwoven." John said, seemingly thoughtful and inspired.

"Thanks, John. Let's grab a Guinness. My mouth is dry from all that talking," I said, half-joking.

We walked out of the venue into the bustling street and sat down on the scratched wooden bench. As we waited for our taxi to take us back to the hotel, a figure walked towards us –a slim woman with long dark glistening hair and chocolate eyes. "I liked your speech. It was kind of cool. Do you happen to have a number for a local taxi company?" she said in an undistinguishable accent as she lent in.

"We're actually waiting for a cab now. Where are you going? Perhaps you can jump in with us?" said John quickly, trying to be helpful.

"No? Are you sure? That's kind. I'm just killing time, my flights this evening and I have a few hours till then, so if you're headed towards Grafton street or somewhere near, I'll jump out there, check out some shops." She replied.

"We're going to the temple bar area for a few 'Guinness' if you wanna join us?" said John in his best Irish Accent. I looked at John and rolled my eyes. It was meant to be us having a Guinness after the talk. It would be a chance to go through the speech and explain the points in more depth. After all, sales and marketing strategy was what he wanted my support with.

"Sure, why not. I mean I'm more of a Vodka or espresso Martini kind of girl. But 'when in Rome," she said, pulling a sideway-smile face in jest. "I'm Nancy, by the way," she said, offering her hand for John to shake.

"You don't seem like a Nancy? You're not a James Bond villain girl, are you?" John said, pretending to whisper.

"I couldn't possibly tell you that, could I? No, I actually get that a fair bit with the name, I'm Swedish, but my nan's English friend, who helped her when my grandpop was sick, was called that. So I kind of got given the name from there, she was from Liverpool, I think, like the soccer team," She explained.

The tattooed bartender pulled the third pint and placed it in front of John, "Cheers broda" he said as he nodded. The sound of guitar music and laughing all around felt like a friendly wall of Irish charm, as strangers, both local and other nationalities, shared the memories they were making. Yet, with all the young and free-willed ambience, living for the day, I felt withdrawn and reflective thinking of my partner Paige and my son Xavier back home. That feeling of being amongst friends and company yet feeling so alone came over me as I stood at the bar watching the world doing its thing. I looked at John, "Hey man. I'm sorry to be a killjoy, but I'm going to have to bail, I've got a banging headache, and I've got some quotes I need to get to clients" I said, tipping my head.

"No, no, I understand. No worries. I'll stay for a few, I know this sounds crazy, but you know when you know? Well, I think I'm in love," he said, looking flustered.

"Oh-kay, well, just be careful, 007. If you need anything, just give me a call." I said, smiling but serious.

John was an interesting character. While I didn't know him that well, he didn't seem the most streetwise type. But I was certain he'd be fine and have a few pints and get back to the hotel an hour or two later.

My alarm went off. 'Oh my god,' I thought to myself, I had forgotten to set my alarm an hour early to get to the airport. I called a taxi and explained I was in a rush. I worked out I could still make it, as long as the taxi arrived within the next few minutes. Luckily, the taxi pulled up, and I jumped in, bag in tow. "To the airport, please," I announced, promptly. 'Shit' I thought, was John waiting on me to share the taxi or had he gone ahead? I wondered. I tried to call his mobile, but it went to voicemail, 'he must have gone to the airport, assuming I'd headed there early' I thought. "Hi John, I'm running late, see you in a bit" I text. I looked at the message John sent last night at 11.45pm, 'one great night,' it simply said. If John had been drinking all that time, maybe he had missed his alarm clock too, I thought. I called him a second time, a little worried but assuring myself nothing was wrong.

"Hey" said a soft voice,

"John?" I said, perplexed by the tone.

"No, it's Nancy. I missed my flight." she said.

"Ah I see okay, I'm sorry to hear that. Can you let John know I called? If you could get him to drop me a call or a text later, that would be great," I said, a little taken back on the situation. Perhaps I'd miscalculated John.

I opened the car door as my phone vibrated, with a text from John. It read, 'I'm sorry. Long story, great night! Nancy missed flight! I offered her my room and slept on the couch. We both fly back tomorrow."

WORDS TO SELL BY

"*I*'ve got a John Daniels on the line if you want to take the call," said my PA, Melissa, "Sure, put him through. Thanks, Mel," I said as I stretched out in my black leather chair, looking out of my office window.

"John, it's been a week. How's things? We never really got time to catch up since Dublin," I said in a questioning tone.

"I know we'd agreed for me to head in tomorrow for another day, but my cousin died Monday and quite honestly, I'm in pieces. Adam was like my best friend. Brothers even, I, I...' He stuttered, breaking down.

"I'm really sorry. I hope you're okay. Don't worry about tomorrow, let's pick up when you're ready" I replied, feeling for him and yet not knowing the words to say.

"Nancy, she had to re-book her connecting flight from London, home to Stockholm. So, I said she could crash at mine, and this happens. She's not left. She picked me up, made me food, made me eat. She's held me in her arms. She even cried, wiping my tears away, telling me she wished she could take my pain away. I'm a mess right now, but I knew it, she's my girl. I'm in love with her." He said, with a cracked voice, notably choked with emotion.

"That's amazing. You two certainly looked like you hit it off in the bar. I'm happy for you, mate," I said, trying to keep the conversation positive.

"Yeah, I'm a bit out of balance with stuff now. I need to get back in the office and work, but it will take me a few days. I'll reschedule for us to catch up on email later, though I know you have probably prepared a lot to go through today. So I'm more than happy if you want to send it over to me on email instead." He said, trying to refocus himself.

"Sure, I'll put these slides I've written on sales email copy and ad writing in a video presentation for you. I'll get one of my team to do it and send it over. I'm thinking of you mate, take it easy and catch up in a few days. Take care. Bye," I said, as I put the phone down.

Sometimes when we lose loved ones, we lose ourselves for a moment. The pain holds us back. It reminds me of how precious life is and how little time we have on this planet to make a difference or experience life. I knew John was hurting, but despite that fact, he still had that point of direction that knew he needed to pull through and get back to work. Nancy, there by his side, really made a difference to him, and I believe he'd have been in a worse place had she not be there to pick him up. Its all too commonly said, but I truly believe that it's the tough times that do indeed show you who is there and who cares. There have been points in my own journey where I have hit rock bottom. But my partner, Paige, has lifted me up, and now our son is here. As he grows each day and looks at me, he gives me purpose and inspiration.

I wrote an article for High Profile magazine last month about love and, I referenced a chapter in the bible, I would not classify myself as religious, but it still speaks volumes to me. "If I have the gift of prophecy and know all mysteries and all knowledge; and if I have all faith, so as to remove mountains, but don't have love, I am nothing." (1 Corinthians 13:2) – it's so true, this journey John is on to turn his company around and start selling, means nothing if it's not for love. Love gives us a reason. Our family, our friends, our partner, perhaps the greatest driver of all is the need to have a purpose. When I was younger, I wanted to be rich, I wanted to be successful, but it was a materialistic viewpoint. I thought if I achieve this or buy that, it will say this about me and while then in my youth, I didn't see the psychology behind it, I retrospectively look back now and see I had my judgement back to front. Today, I push forward to build more success to give and be more than myself. Ultimately, when you have love and find acceptance with that, you look beyond and see that the true gift is in giving back.

After a reflective, introverted moment and grabbing a coffee, I got my head together and started to work on the sales email and ad copy. After all, I'd set the day out to go through it with John.

I put together the following slides and advice for John.

HOW DO YOU WRITE THE PERFECT EMAIL?

How do you write the perfect sales email? Well, there's is no perfect way. There are many not to do's, of course, like being 'too sales' or seen as 'spam,' but really people are different, and what works for one person might not for another. There, however, are tricks that, in the majority of cases, tend to create results.

The first is to make sure you use the prospects first name. Again, like selling on the phone, you don't want to use it too much, just once or twice if you're counting the subject title too. That's right, using the prospects name in the subject title can work well. Why? Because it looks personal, and it catches the prospects eye.

The second super important thing to bear in mind is to be personal. Try not to seem like you've written a generic email that has been sent out in mass. By customizing aspects like their company name, and even putting in a personal line or two, whether it's something you've seen on their LinkedIn or website or something about their company in the news or online. Saying that, please make sure it's not cheesy. If it's too corny, then it will be a nonstarter. Be subtle, and it will make them think you've taken your time to reach out.

This is also hugely important. Like a sales call, you need to get to the point, don't waffle. Be precise and explain why you're emailing, and as simply as possible, try to convey the value you are looking to add with your offering. The more direct and relative to the prospect you can make it, the more impactful.

Don't be scared to try different things, different styles of pitch. One great advantage you have with email is the ability to test. If you are using an email marketing tool, you can a/b test, which means using two different email templates and testing, which has a better hit rate or conversion or opened and read rate.

Lastly, don't forget to close. Just because you're not on the phone, don't leave it open and wishy-washy. End with a suggested action. Ask for a convenient time to call or ask for their feedback. Great sales emails, get replies, and engagement.

AD COPY THAT WORKS.

When it comes to writing ads, you need to go back to knowing your customer and profiling them. Think about who the ads are being written to attract or engage.

Writing sales copy is all about pitching the point as possible, with simple yet powerful words. When you are writing adverts, to close with the desired effect, you need to suggest action. Whether you are looking for the prospect to click through and buy the offer or fill out their details, you need to put forward the action they need to take.

One major don't is to try being too clever or imaginative. If you're marketing a consumer product, then sure, if you have a huge budget and want to get people talking, be different, be shocking. If you're a business-to-business brand, you want to stay within the guidelines with a business offering or a small consumer brand. Stick to creating simple copy that informs, promotes, and creates actions. It's all about return on investment (ROI).

Like email, marketing is good practice for online advertising on a platform like Facebook using a/b testing. It's important that when you have created your ad, you create a few different options.

Facebook will let you create dynamic ads. This goes one above a/b testing, allowing you to have several options for your headline, body copy, and Call-to-action (CTA) – this is the text or suggestion you have to get the prospect to take action, to click through and do as you suggest.

The best thing about this is that Facebook will work out the best combination that works and use it to promote. You can be the best sales copywriter in the world, but you can't beat, actively testing and putting into play the results.

When it comes to writing good sales copy, people tend to overthink, like making a sales call.

THE BEST LEAD GENERATING PLATFORMS

Facebook – I'd say personally Facebook is my favorite platform to advertise on. It has a wealth of tools and performs better for me. It has the dynamic ads feature and is fairly simple and self-explanatory to setup. Of course, you can go into depth with it, and it can be fairly advance if you use some of the real enriching features. But if you want to run a simple campaign, it's great.

Instagram – Instagram owned by Facebook allows you to create a simple ad on the platform directly or have a Facebook ad that runs across the two platforms, depending on your audience. This is a good option, though more people have Facebook than Instagram, and Instagram tends to have a younger audience.

LinkedIn – LinkedIn is good, though it does tend to work out pricier than Facebook. What is better about LinkedIn is the job titles are built more directly than with Facebook. LinkedIn is a business social media platform created so that it is more conducive to selling to people in a certain role/position.

Google Ads – You often see the sponsored matches in Google, suggested at the top of the search. People pay for them to be there, and there's a good reason, so people click through. If people are searching for something, where better to be than in the top results. Google is good, but as I mentioned before, you need to tangibly know who is visiting your website because if your website doesn't convert, you have a problem, and your ROI won't be great.

YouTube – This is a great tool to use if you have a message or want a different touchpoint or way of connecting with your prospects. After all, video and media and the internet are getting more enriched by the day, and if you're anything like me, and the growing trend of young people, you may well watch YouTube more than you actually watch tv. It's a good platform, but again it leads all traffic to your website. You need to make sure that the website converts, so you are using the best analytical solutions out there to ascertain who's been visiting, so you can connect and close.

Others – Of course, there are many other platforms, I've not mentioned, that are also great, and as the years go on, there will be new leaders that offer affordable advertising solutions. It is important to review and try new things by way of online lead generation. But when you find something that works, a platform that creates results double down.

I clicked 'send' and shut my laptop. Hopefully, these pointers would give John some food for thought, and he could build this into his new sales strategy. Sales funnels are super effective, but it's often a case of trial and error. Each company and offering are different, and so is the audience and prospective buyers, so you need to try, adapt, and test and double down.

Having a good sales funnel, or even a few different sales funnels running, can be the difference between a business on its knees or a business booming. I know this first-hand. While I'm a 'sales and marketing expert' running a Lead genera-tion agency, I actually implement this for us directly.

If you want to drive sales, you need to put in the work and the investment and time needed to build a solid foundation. If you want to build a beautiful home, you have to first make sure the footing is sound, then you can build with confiden-ce.

I walked out of my office and into the main office, "Right guys, how are we doing today? Give me a sum up, Chandler," I said, pointing over to our team leader.

"Yes, we're doing okay. We're a bit down on results from last week, but its Friday," he said in reply.

"No one's waiting for you to knock on their door and ask if they want something. It doesn't matter what day it is, or time for that matter. Do you think CEOs think, 'oh wait, its Friday, I'll shut off today or go shopping?" no, they are working. Guys, just because its Friday, don't go soppy on me. Pull it out the bag!' I said, assertively hitting my hand against the other in gesticulation.

Sometimes I find myself being tough with my words, but to hit home and motivate my team, to create winners that go above and beyond, you need to split the weak from the rough.

A LITTLE INSPIRATION

*M*y mobile vibrated, and a text came through, 'Sale,' it said. I unlocked my phone; it was from John. It had been a couple weeks since I'd last heard from him. I called him immediately.

"Amazing, congratulations. Tell me..." I demanded, excited to hear the good news.

"Yeah, so me and my team, Sid, and Barry, sat down. I talked them through the sales strategy I'd drawn out, as you suggested, with the different steps. We put an ad campaign together that started to build some leads, and with the basic script you gave me, I built our own sales script and followed your guideline. And they went for it. They've signed up for 12 months!" he said, in an excited rush.

"You know what to do now. You have them onboard, your offering is great, use that sales strategy, that sales funnel and double down. Get more leads in and more sales closed. It's a numbers game, as cliché as that sounds, it's the truest thing in sales," I said, through a smile that had adorned my face.

Its moments like this that really make what I do worthwhile. Helping to create results, but more than that, helping people to create results for themselves.

"I'm actually near your office this afternoon. I've got a meeting at lunchtime. Why don't I pop in?" I suggested.

"Yes, that would be great. See you this afternoon." John said.

I walked up to the run-down office block. There was graffiti all up the wall and a woman outside smoking a roll-up cigarette. "Sorry, could you tell me the way to Zem AI," I said to the lady as she blew a cloud of smoke at the tree in front of her.

"Yeah, it's the last one on the left, love. All colours and that on the signage," she said, waving her free hand in a circular motion.

"Thanks," I said, as I lifted my eyebrows in acknowledgement.

As I walked down the corridor, I heard 'YES' shouted out. It sounded like John. I knocked on the aged red door with the Zem Ai logo on. "Hello," I said, pushing on the door. "Another one," John said, grinning, with his thumbs up.

"Another sale? You're on a roll." I said, congratulating him. John took my hand as I approached and shook it up and down. "Thank you. Really, thank you," he said, looking me in the eyes.

"John, it's all on you, buddy. You're doing it. I gave you direct guidelines, but you choose to take the steps. You choose to come to me, to learn about sales, and that's what we've done. Look at strategy, pitch, and the rest. That's what makes an entrepreneur. You might not be an expert in all aspects of business, but you seek, find, draw resources together. That's what the best do. There's more that we can do together, but you've got it started." I said.

"You have to try some of these," John said, passing me a tub of biscuits. "Nancy made them. They're cinnamon and ginger biscuits. I think they're a Swedish thing, but they're lovely," he said as he took a bite of the one in his hand.

"Wait, Nancy? You're... she...," I stuttered.

"I asked her to stay. It just felt ... with all that happened, that fate had aligned the passing stars, and we are somehow ... we've found each other; I believe in that stuff somehow. Everything happens for a reason and all that." He said, looking to the side in a daze, drawing on his feelings.

"No, I totally get that you both seemed to resonate on the same frequency when you met. I'm happy for you. Don't let it, let you drop the ball though, this business has feet," I said, drawing the conversation to a focus point.

"Let's grab a coffee, and I'll introduce you to the team," he said, pointing to the kettle in the corner of the room.

As we walked over to the other side of the office, two faces looked up from their desks with beaming smiles. Sid a slim 19-year-old lad in the tightest check suit you could buy, with a gelled quiff and skin faded sides. The other, Barry, a large-framed gentleman in his late 40s, with a short-sleeve shirt and wispy hair.

"Hey, it's so cool to finally meet you. John's been talking about everything you've shown him and got us reading some of your blogs and stuff. I'm like really on this sales thing bigtime," said Sid, in an overconfident manner, clearly hiding his nerves.

"Barry," said Barry, holding out his hand, obviously a man of few words.

"Nice to meet you both. John tells me good things. This is the team that's going to make stirs in the sector, I can tell," I said, grabbing a seat. "So, first of all, I'm sure you think I'm going to talk about sales, but I wanna know what inspires you all. Tell me, guys, what are your goals?" I said, looking at Sid, John, and Barry.

"I wanna go to Ibiza with my mates and get a Rolex, that's me, baller," said Sid excitedly.

"Check this out," I said as I took off my watch and handed it to him.

"Wow," he said, putting it on his wrist.

"The only thing between you and that watch is 'you.' You want it, you can. Work your arse off, and when you get it, it feels so damn good. Well, until you want the next thing. But that's a different story," I said, joking.

"My goal is to travel more. Maybe have kids. Just have a good life, not wanting for anything because I can buy it," Said John, looking at the team.

"I want my ex back. I wanna prove to her I can provide for her and my girl, Eliza, and take them to Disney land," said Barry looking sad.

"Let me tell you something now; YOU can! It's funny, usually when I do this with my team, and we get newbies starting, there's always one idiot that says, 'I wanna be an astronaut,' and I'm like, why the hell are you sitting here then? No, you all have goals that you're going to smash. They are achievable. What I want you to do is go home this evening and make an image of your goal. There are a few ways you can do that, you can save images on your phone from online and make a collage, or you can get magazines and cut-out pictures and stick them together. I want you to make the image because the clearer you can see it, feel it, smell and taste it. The more real it is to you, the closer it is. And when you have your image, burn it into your memory so that you can see it when you close your eyes. If you relax enough, you're there." I said to the team.

I truly believe in the power of focusing on what you want to achieve. Some people call this manifesting or willing the universe to give it to you. Quite honestly, regardless of what you call it, it does work to a degree. Of course, you can't be a billionaire tomorrow, but you can will it long-term and actionably follow steps toward getting there, and who knows what you can achieve if you try hard enough. Everything in this world is numeric, wealth, money. It's all just numbers. It's the value that we give out which determines the yield we receive, and as you move toward building or amounting wealth, you see the niches, sectors and areas this is most true, and you hone in.

It's one thing to have goals and vision, but it's important to have a sense of self and to believe that you truly deserve that for which you are asking. Your reason, your vision, should be in the vein of good and backed by purpose, then you truly can believe you deserve it because you know your end goal involves giving back

As we spoke back and forth about our goals, I could see the team getting excited and working out how many sales they needed to earn what they desired. "This is it; you see what you want, and you work out how to get it, and then you do it. You 'Think it, Pitch it, Sell it,' that's how you get what you want." I said, feeling inspired myself.

"And how about this, this sales stuff. I'm going to make it easier for you. I'm going to introduce you to the combination that makes getting sales easier and faster." I said, getting out my laptop and placing it on the table.

I opened up a training presentation I created for the session and moved my laptop to the center of the table so everyone could see the screen.

The SSS Combination – The 3 S of sales success! It read across the screen.

Sales funnel – Hopefully, now you have a good idea of what a sales funnel is and how it generates warm leads online.

Systemize – What does this mean? Everything needs to be flowing and automated. When someone fills in a form in your sales funnel, it automatically needs to generate an email. It needs to update your CRM system and notify you. Systemizing processes are not just a sales thing either. It can be systematic, invoicing, or all different applications. You need to look at processes within the business that you can automate with software or solutions. The less you have to do, the better systemized you are. There are so many great tools out there that will help you with this. For example, rather than send emails back and forth with a prospect, send them a link to your calendar with a scheduling tool. This will cut the need to go back and forth, and it will book a meeting in your calendar when a prospect books it. Systemizing can also be looking at things like nurturing. The email automation part of your sales strategy, for the leads you don't close, you need to keep them warm and nurture them. This can be done with very little effort when it's all set up.

Lastly.

Solutions – You're currently working on spreadsheets trying to keep track of call-backs. You need a CRM; this stands for Contact Management System. It makes sure you are calling the prospects back at the right time and staying on top of your to-do list.

With the SSS combination, you can automate so much. You can create leads online, nurture them, engage with them, note it down, all the way through, from sending proposals and sending invoices, even onboarding.

To get this right, you need to divide your business into three sections on paper. 1. Sales 2. Delivery, and 3. After-service. Look at what each part of your business entails and look for solutions that work to make each task easier. When you are looking for solutions, they need to be cost-effective and have a definitive job in place. Systemizing and solution should make your life easier, not harder, so you don't need it if it doesn't simplify or increase results.

The business should be like a machine –your key part is operation. You engage with clients and keep it all together. With systems and solutions in place to help you send proposals quicker, nurture prospects, schedule meetings, and so much more, you can focus on driving sales.

"It makes a lot of sense, and oddly our software, Zem AI, as we grow, will tell us more from the data too as we onboard more clients. It's like a loop or a flywheel. We put feedback in constantly, and the whole thing runs smoother and better and that snowballs," said John, excited.

"Exactly," I said, smiling, "You're making sales now. Imagine the setup to allow you to really increase input and output," I said.

TELLERS OF THE SECRET FUTURE

The letterbox snapped as the postman put the letters through the door. I picked up the post, and amongst the bills, and junk mail, I saw a matte black square envelope with a '2F1' logo inscribed on the back. 'Hmm,' I thought, looking at it. I happen to like nice, artistically crafted marketing materials. I carefully opened up the envelope and inside was a matte black card which read, "You are selected to join us next Friday evening. You will be messaged the location and time details shortly after opening this letter. See you soon 2F1"

"What is this?" I said aloud. My phone vibrated. I'd received a message reading 'Green park tube (Piccadilly exit, southside) 20:00.' This is a great joke or advertising stunt, I thought, putting my phone into my pocket.

Thinking over and over, not mentioning this to anyone, I made my excuses and told my partner I had a business meeting. Sitting on the train, I felt an edge of nerves. Something I haven't felt in a while. Was this the right thing to do? What could it be? Surely, it was some joke from a friend or an invite to a well-marketed event, I thought as my stomach turned.

It was dark as I exited the tube station, as directed in the text. There were all kinds of people walking in a million directions, going about their evening. I stepped to the side, waiting for someone to approach me and tell me I'd been pranked, but my phone vibrated. The text read, 'there's a black Maybach waiting at the entrance of the Ritz Hotel, 770 feet away from you. Don't talk to anyone. Just open the door and get in.' My mind was running overtime, and my stomach had butterflies. What was this? My intrigue overcame my nerves, and I made my way to the hotel entrance, looking around me as I walked to see I wasn't being followed or watched. There, slightly back from the entrance, was a blacked-out Maybach. I opened the door, and the driver partition was up, so I couldn't see the driver, but the car began to move. Another vibration and a message said, 'on the seat, there is a black blindfold, put it on. Don't worry, it's all okay. Place your trust in us.' By now, I was feeling hot and cold with nerves. Should I get out of the car and get out of there? Or should I go with it? After all, it was some expensive joke, I assumed. I put on the blindfold with a big breath in. If I were being kidnapped, would it be like this? I wondered. Surely it wouldn't feel as optional as this, and it would be more forced? I questioned myself.

Time was going slowly, but I guessed 10 minutes had passed so far. Suddenly, I felt the car go down as if we were driving down a tunnel. My ears popped, and my phone vibrated. I peered out from my blindfold and looked, 'you can remove your blindfold. I'll be there shortly,' read the text, shortly before the signal went. We were driving down a tunnel, underground, I'd guessed. What was going on? I felt my heart in my chest, and my mind went still.

The car stopped, and the driver got out and opened the door for me, "Welcome to 2F1, sir," he said, removing his hat. I'll take you inside and introduce you.

As we walked through the doorway, I saw a group of men sitting around a large meeting table. One of the men got up and walked towards me, with his hand out, "Anthony." He said, introducing himself, "nice to meet you. I'm sorry we've gone to this extreme to meet you, but I'll explain. This organization, society, say as you will, is a private collective of individuals with a vested interest in the future. We do so to make sure our families prosper and that they are safe and protected. To do that, we positively and objectively look at the future. We're not a cult, we're not 'the Illuminati,' and we don't directly impact or affect politics, local or international. Simply put, we are a group of men, as you see before you today, acting in our own best interests, and we would like to welcome you into our club." He said, looking at me square in the eyes with complete certainty.

"But why me? I'm just a sales guy with a sales company," I said, confused.

"Don't be so humble. You're an entrepreneur. You think differently from most. We know you're thinking like a 2F1 member. Don't take this the wrong way, but we collectively invest in technology to predict but also to understand. One solution we have uses algorithms to connect us with individuals who are actively operating or thinking in a multitude of fields we are interested in. For example, Blockchain, cryptocurrency. How are you doing on that?" he said, now with a softer gaze.

"Yes, I'm doing okay. I'm a little invested in Bitcoin, Ethereum. How do you know?" I said, concerned.

"Software," he said, smiling. "Data tells us everything. Like history, it helps us navigate challenges today by applying knowledge from the past. It acts as an artificial experience. While we might not know something, we can count on our data lead gut to move forward." He said, reading my facial expression for feedback.

"So, you brought me here because I have a few bitcoin?" I questioned.

"I brought you here because we know you're as fascinated about the future as we are. We know how much you search online for new cutting-edge technologies. We know you're creative, introverted, yet able to act responsibly and morally in opportunities of power. But most importantly, you're a communicator. On top of all this, we need new blood. New members, I mean. Not in a vampire way, you know what I mean," he said jokingly.

"So, what do you want from me?" I asked.

"We want you to join us. To sit in a meeting when we discuss new ideas, technologies, their implications, and positives. And for this, you get direction, practical and investable advice. Making money is easy when you have a good idea of what lies ahead. If you need mentorship, we're here too. All we ask is that you abide by five key rules.

1) You can talk about the group, but if you do, don't use the name, change it. In relation to members, don't say 'who' and 'where'. You don't talk about members names, and you never say where we meet or when. 2fl, the name it's out there. People have heard about it as a myth, and

so that is fine. In fact, it's kind of fun. People think so much more into it, but so long as we are protecting the core, that's all we ask.

2) We're not about favors. We're not a club of scratch my back, and I'll scratch yours. Therefore, we don't directly ask favors of other members. Sure, members can do business, but that's private and separate. It gets too complicated when members owe each other favors.

3) It's personal, but it's not personal. Basically, we get to know each other well, but we don't talk about family. The reason is, it gets in the way and adds complications. When we meet, we meet as individuals. While what we do and what we discuss is directly applicable to the long-term value of our families.

4) Don't use our intelligence for bad. Line your pockets, invest, build, and advance, sure, but don't take our advice and collectively discuss it to incriminate, morally inconvenience or take advantage of the rest of the

world. We join as one to better the world and our families lives for the future.

5) Spread the word, not directly, but in your everyday role. Share wisdom and help people with the adoption of new ideas and technologies. Be an advocate for positive change," he said, looking at me.

"Sounds good to me. What's next?" I asked, interested but still a little apprehensive.

"Let me take you in to meet everyone, and we'll give you a rundown on some of the new areas and technology that's in front of us. We'll end the session by explaining what 2F1 stands for and it's a superpower. We then explain how you can actively use every day to grow your business and advise others in doing so, but also, it's a tool that might help you plan in life also." He said, gesturing to me to walk towards the table of members.

As I walked up to the table and looked at the faces emerging, I was surprised to see a few faces I recognized—the members were all smartly dressed, mostly in black, sympathetic perhaps to the club colors. As I looked around the table and introduced myself, member by member nodded and said their name. A few I didn't need announcing, but I was surprised at their humble attitude toward doing so. As if I didn't know who they were. It was amazing to be in a hub of individuals that had all left their personal baggage at the door and spoke as equals.

That evening my mind was opened to the future, to tomorrows normal. Which, to me, while comprehensible, I found amazing.

I was told about the emergence of new business capitals in less economically developed areas, to the migration of people from oversaturated western cities, to the spread of geographic hubs worldwide more equally. With hubs being interlinked by tunnels and highspeed shoots.

With regards to money, I was told about the forthcoming mass adoption of cryptocurrency on mobile phones held virtual wallets with increase traceability and government subsidy payments, new laws, and centralized taxation.

I was told how renewable energy, mainly solar, built into the most applicable buildings and cars.

I was told about farming and food manufacturing, with sideways grown, stacked fruit and veg to synthetic grown healthy meats to substitute today's process.

It was revealed to me how health would dramatically change with personalized diets based on DNA and quantum devices to support the body consistent health tracking with technology, wearables, and more knowledge into eating habits.

We would live in a world where a majority of the habitants were no longer employed directly in roles as AI, and robotics had taken most of these positions but now rewarded in the use of new platforms where they are paid for their interaction and viewing. From visual entertainment to virtual gaming, users will be rewarded for their behavior, sociality, and buying actions.

All this possibility amazed me. While a great deal of it seemed plausible and near, the overall connection painted a strange, somewhat scary future. But then again, as suggested to me by one of the members, if our ancestors, only a mere few generations ago, looked at today, they would be in for a shock.

"Now, let me explain our name, and it really is straight forward. 2f1, we believe in finding two solutions to one problem or looking at two possibilities leading to one outcome. So take the monitory situation at the moment. The US dollar is massively inflated, and well, people in the know are losing faith in fiat money (paper-based, gold-backed, government printed money), so the future is unlikely to be paper-based. One option is that Bitcoin, the number one in cryptocurrency, is the new gold and stands to have a new system built on it that is transitioned in. Another option is that governments create their own digital currencies, beginning with Central Bank Digital Currencies (CBDC). For each and every predicted change to come about, there are multiple ways to get there. By understanding how these changes play out, we align a strategy to be both protected and at the forefront. Take something like this. It's not all about the money. Its protection. For example, with the dollar and other fiat currencies failing at the moment, large companies are actually losing, as their cash reserves don't make money, but their value goes down. So by having a vested interest or staking some of the cash reserves into Bitcoin, for example, we are adapting to what will inevitably happen. This 2 to 1 strategy can also be applied to business. For example, as you know, multiple platforms do the same thing with selling online, but one will likely give you the best return. So you split your advertising spend between Facebook and Google ads to achieve the same outcome. When you see one delivering better, you go with that one and double down. 2f1 is an approach to life. A woman might date two guys to find who her better half is to be. It plays out in a million different ways, it's not quite the Fibonacci sequence, but it works for us." He reveals with a smile.

"You've opened my mind, I have to say, and I really like the 2f1 strategy. I'll work that into things this week and see how I go," I said, thanking him.

"Right, that's it. Hope you've enjoyed your first meeting. We meet quarterly; we'll keep you posted on the next event.

Download this app," he said, pointing to his phone. "It looks like a random photo editing app, right? But you hold your finger on the app for five seconds, and it asks you for a password. Put in 2fl, and it opens a list of topics to read up on. Meeting dates will always be texted to you a day before."

"Do I go to the Ritz again and take the car?' I said, wondering. "No, follow me up the stairs. There are four exits, all that go to different parts of London, from Westminster to Mayfair, Kensington to Bank," he revealed.

"Wow, that's amazing," I said, astonished. "Yes, it was built back in wartime, but we use it now. Head up the stairs and take the first door to the left. It will take you back to the roundabout where you got picked up. The other doors have a fair walk built-in," he said, laughing.

I followed four flights of stairs up until I got to the top, where I saw five doors. I took the first door to the left. I walked for what seemed like five minutes until I saw a lift at the end of the corridor. I pressed 'G' for ground, and the lift started to move. The door opened, and I was in a hotel foyer. I looked back at the buttons. There was no floor below ground, just G and the upper levels. I smiled.

As I travelled home, I thought about that night. How privy to the information I'd been, and what an honour it had been to have been brought into this. I thought about the 2f1 strategy and what it might mean to the decisions I would make and the advice I would give going forward. The future was there for the taking.

ANOTHER CROSSROADS

The sound of the crystal aqua blue Aegean Sea kissing the shore soothed me as I sipped an ice-cold mythos beer. Time to relax after a focused quarter with my group of agencies. The offices were all doing well, and now it was 'me time', 'family time'. My partner, Paige, made sandcastles in the sand with our little boy, Xavier. Their white, blonde hair beaming, bright in the sunshine, and the sound of her talking and him laughing filled me with happiness.

My phone vibrated. I had tried not to keep my phone on so much this trip, but today I was waiting on confirmation of an investment I had emailed to me. I opened the message 'They want to buy me out,' it read. It was from John.

'What do you mean?' I replied.

My phone rang, it was John. "Hi, John. How are things?" I said in anticipation.

"I've had an email from a company wanting to buy Zem AI. I don't know what to do. I'm hesitant to sell, but then I'm interested to hear them out," he said nervously.

"I think you've answered your own question there. You have to do what you think is right," I suggested.

"I don't know. We've grown so fast these last few months, especially. We have almost 300 subscribed customers now. Paying on average £850 a month. We're looking to turn over 3 million this year." He said proudly.

"That's amazing. Just think, if you can grow that in the time you have, imagine what it could turn over in five years. Ten years even. You could grow the company and float it. Sell some of your shares and focus on you." I said encouragingly.

"It's just... I was thinking last night when I got the email. I walked into the garden, Nancy was in the bath, and I just looked up at the stars. And I thought about what you had previously said about business. About how you can often reverse engineer the end result to see how you get there, and so I thought, what actually do I want from life? Sure, I can grow the business or even, like you say, do something like an IPO (Initial public offering), but why? Surely, selling and growing and selling is just a difference in number, right?" he said, opening up.

As I looked at my family, smiling at me and eating their ice creams, I said, "Yes, there's more to life than a few more zeros. You have to think about your life. What you want ultimately. As I'm sure you've heard the expression 'Life's not about finding a destination, it's about enjoying the journey,' and I'd go so far as to say that life's not even a journey. It's more like a piece of music. Every aspect, the begining, the chorus, the breakdown or middle eight, and even the last big outro-chorus, it's all there to be enjoyed and experienced. Too many people hate their life. Hate the sound of their own song. They don't realise they can re-pitch, pardon the pun, and change. So I guess the question is, are you happy? Does Zem AI make you happy?" I said, laying back looking at the sky.

"You always seem to have the right balance when I think about it. You have your agency group, and you do that well. But you travel all the time, and you seem to have it right." He said, almost inquisitively.

"I guess I believe in the concept of lifestyle design. It's an idea brought up in a few books I read some time back. Of course, you need to have a sense of purpose, and you need to have money coming in, but if you can build a company and use leverage to free yourself out of full-time management, then you can decide to pick and choose and live a life that excites you. For me, it's picking up and heading off to places. I think there's so much in travel, exploring other cultures and seeing the world." I said, watching Xavier, who now had ice cream running down his chin.

"Zem AI has been my life now for the best part of a year. Yes, it has really started to take shape and make results this year. But the build-up, the work that's gone in. I appreciate if I do sell, then I've been very lucky and fortunate. Many people never have the opportunity to grow an idea, build it into a business, and sell it." He said, reflecting.

"Yes, its hard work. Most people think it's an overnight success, but they don't see the hard graft, learning, developing, and hustle that goes into getting something to work. Our journey, the sales side of things, is just the butter on the bread. You had the bread, the idea and the focus, I gave you the butter, and you filled it with cheese, ham and lettuce." I said.

"Don't. You're making me hungry," he joked. "Isn't what you did more like me making the sandwich and finding people to eat it?" he suggested.

"Each way you look at it, Zem AI is a big juicy sandwich right now, and these guys obviously want more than a bite." I joked back. "Tell me, anyway. Who are they?" I asked.

"A competitor. I think they want to buy us to get us out of the market. We're growing quickly, and I don't know that they like it," He said.

"Don't forget, it's also your technology, your client base and your team. They are buying so much more," I said. "It's a very typical way to grow and dominate a vertical in the area of technology. If a big name sees a start-up or a potential rival on the horizon, they buy you out if they like their technology and want their client base. Remember, they no doubt want you more than you want them." I told him. "The next step would be to sign some kind of confidentiality agreement, so neither party could discuss the conversation at this stage. Then they would likely want to see the financials and come in to see the business to do their due diligence."

"That's fine. The big thing that scares me is if I sell if the price is right and I sleep on it, and I think yes, what's going to happen to the team? I know its dog eat dog in business, but these guys are most of the reason we've boomed. They have put their time in, and it's altered their lives. Some of the newbies have even given up other job opportunities to come onboard. Sid and Barry, it changed their lives, almost as much as mine. The business and the growth we have all been through. Sid is, well, Sid. But he's loving life. He's got a new apartment, car, and girlfriend. Living every young man's dream and Barry, he's reclaimed his life, from being in a rut to turning things around with his partner. I can't take that from them for all the money in the world. It wouldn't be right. I wouldn't live with that guilt." He said, concerned.

"If you sell, you can make clauses in the contract. Terms that have to be abided by as part of the sale. I'm not a legal expert, by any stretch of the imagination, but I'm almost certain that can be done fairly easily. You can agree that all the staff stay on, in their existing roles." I suggested, scratching my head.

Paige walked over, Xavier following behind, and handed me a delicious smelling souvlaki Gyros pita, with crispy fat pork, dollops of tzatziki, overflowing with onions.

"Your right. I need to think this over, but as always, thank you." I said, pondering his words.

"mmm." I said, with my mouth full, "mmyeah," I tried to pronounce.

"Are you eating?" John said, laughing.

"Yes," I said, "sorry, I'm chewing on one naughty Greek kebab. It's amazing." I said, finishing the rest of my mouthful.

"I thought the dial tone was international. Whereabouts are you?" he questioned.

"Ios. It's a tiny little island in the Cyclades group of islands in Greece. It's lovely here. You should come here with Nancy. It's chilled. Nice little bar scene, and it's got some cool little hotels with trendy suites and villas with pools overlooking the sea."

"Sounds amazing. I'll definitely add that to my travel itinerary. Right, I'm going to head out for lunch. My stomach is practically eating itself. I'm so hungry now. Catch up later."

"John, before you go, think about this. A wise gentleman once told me the 2f1 approach, a way of thinking. Look at two ways to achieve one future vision, goal, or destination. If you really think about what you want your life to look like, what that image of happiness is, think about the two different directions that lead there. One is not selling, growing it, and getting to where you want to be, and the other is selling it and getting to where you want to be from there. Think about it, what the journey of both means. Perhaps there's a middle way, and you sell some and keep some. I don't know, but the 2f1 thinking approach is a tool to think about things differently. Anyway, I'll let you grab some lunch. The mayo from mine is running down my hand as we speak," I said, laughing. "Bye."

It's moments like this, I realise quite how lucky I am to live a life of freedom. To some people, having a choice and options seems far away. Problems and money hold them back, but I, for one, know by having the right focus, you can turn things around. Travel is an incredible way to open up your mind to see how others live and experience cultural and environmental differences. Travelling gives you the perfect time to reflect, and sometimes while the grass seems greener on the other side, the weather is warmer, the food tastes better, it gives us a moment to reflect and appreciate who we are and where we are from. Travelling not only gives us a feeling of being a world citizen and being at one with all, but it also gives us time for a singularity of self. It gives us a change in focus on that which is important; family, friends, and love.

From struggling to getting an idea to the market, John's journey to now being in a position to have complete freedom was magical to see. While he was torn between options, he had the power. For the first time, he truly had control. This is something which many people don't realise that our own fate is in our hands. We're in the circumstances we are due to the actions and choices we take. Sometimes, while the future can seem bleak, there is hope. There is light at the end of the tunnel. You can change simply by wanting to. No matter what situation you're in, what pressures you have against you, ideas can become a reality. From darkness, we can appreciate the glimmer of light most. In obsession, we can truly feel freedom when we untie ourselves mentally. I'm a big believer in what doesn't kill you makes you stronger.

Knowing John's next steps could change his life was an amazing thought. I put my phone in my bag and pondered, gazing at the tiny thin clouds moving across the sky into the distance.

CLOSED DEAL

Four days later, and I was back in the UK. Rested and replenished with vitality after a perfect week away with the family. John had travelled down to meet me in Hastings, near my seaside residence in East Sussex. We met at a hotel restaurant, with a terrace with views of the sea opposite the pier. John was on tender-hooks, waiting for a response from his potential buyer, knowing correspondence was due any hour now.

Finally, 40 minutes, later after some light conversation, John's phone pinged, "They have come back and said they would like me to give them an asking price for the business," John said, turning to me.

"I'm a sales expert, and while negotiation falls somewhat into that bracket, there's a real art to deal negotiation. My advice would be not to do that." I said promptly.

"What do you mean?" he questioned.

"If you offer up a potential asking price first, they have the upper hand in negotiating down. If you undervalue yourself, they may just accept it. For what its worth, I'd go back and ask them for an offer," I advised him.

"Yeah, that makes a lot of sense. I've thought about it, and I've searched lots online. There are multiple ways you can value a business. I wouldn't have any idea what to ask for," he admitted.

"What do you want? Factoring in that this has to set you up for the next project you might take on, or if you're looking to retire, you'll need a little more. Unless you move overseas and live cheaper," I said, looking at my coffee.

"I'm such at a crossroads. I never quite envisioned I'd be here so soon. Retiring at this age, I mean, I don't know, I think I'd go crazy." He said, looking at his phone.

John's phone made a 'ping' noise, and he quickly unlocked it, opening up the email he was expecting. "They've come back with five million. F**king hell. Five million," he said, in an animated fashion.

"Ask for twelve," I said assertively.

"What? Five million, that's more than I ever imagined," he began.

"You're looking to turn over three million this year, yes? You should be looking for a few more multiples. Suggest four years, which at three million per year would be twelve million."

"I don't know. I mean, it's asking for a lot. What if they say no?" he said, fearful.

"They want your company, and if they are the biggest competitor, they will pay more than that. They know about your turnover. There's major growth in that, and you have to ask for more, with the view to meeting somewhere close to it." I said, looking at a nervous John.

"You're right. I'll ask for twelve million." With that, John took to his phone and wrote a reply, getting straight to the point. His message read, "After careful consideration, I would be looking more toward a figure of twelve million," John sighed. "I hope I haven't blown it," he laughed nervously as he looked at me.

"Have a drink. Take a deep breath. It's done. It's in God's hands, as they say," I said, trying to reassure him.

Ping, his phone went again. He opened it in a rush, "ah no. Sales email," he said. We looked at each other and laughed.

"Bloody salespeople," I said, grinning. He shook his head, smiling. "Look, let's take a walk. Take your mind off of this for a moment." I put £20 on the table and nodded to the waiter.

As we walked down the promenade, you could hear the laughter of children playing and the sound of music in the background as the warm yet British sea breeze floated through the trees in the park.

"So, John. Tell me. Your days, hours, maybe minutes before knowing if you're going to be a millionaire for sure. Cold hard cash. What are you going to do? What's next?" I said as we walked along the street toward the crazy golf and amusement arcades.

"Well, I'm going to ask Nancy to marry me. It's been a whirlwind, but I know she's the one. When I met her, I had maybe £3,000 to my name. If things didn't turn around, I was close to losing it all at one stage. She has never looked at me for money, and she doesn't even know quite how much this may end up being, so it's going to change our lives for sure. She's been there with me through a lot of this. Where, when, I don't know. I'll work that out, but I want it to be magical. But between now and then, I just want to travel. See the world with Nancy. Visit Sweden, go to Asia, explore eastern Europe, and go places I've never even thought about. I don't know what I want to do. I don't know even where we'll live yet. Perhaps I'll get a small apartment in a couple of places and live across them," he said deep in thought.

"You know Portugal is lovely, and they have a non-habitual tax residency program. This means you can live there and not pay tax on your foreign income for ten years, or something like that. Don't quote me, and I'll look into it, but that's an option. I think you only have to be there half the year too. Or Monaco," I suggested.

"No. I'm not the Monaco type. I'm more flip flops than designer boat shoes. It's too overpriced. I want simple. The biggest thing that scares me is I don't know what to do next." He said.

"Well, you have all the time in the world. The rest of your life to decide. Too many people stress and rush into things because they feel they are on a timeline or are being compared to their peers or the Jones' next door. You have the luxury of starting afresh. It's okay not to have a plan. You can't rush a good idea."

"You're right. I do know, what I do next, needs to be around creating a legacy and about giving back, as cliché as that sounds." He said shyly.

"It makes complete sense. Nothing makes sense if there isn't a purpose behind it. That's why I'm going to write a book like you said. Even if I can help a handful of others to better their lives and give them some direction, then it's got to be a good thing."

"Wait, I've got it! 'Think it. Pitch it. Sell it.," he said, smiling.

Later that week, the buyer came back with an agreement to buy the business for 10.5 million. John made sure they had catered to all his requests. Keeping on the team in their existing roles and even giving them a pay increase. Later that year, he set up a foundation, helping budding young tech entrepreneurs to get started. Supporting them with everything from business planning to sales.

Nancy said 'yes', and they planned to marry in two years as an unexpected surprise got in the way of the perfect dress. Nancy was pregnant with John's baby girl.

THANK YOU

*I*f there's one thing that the story shows us is that if you are determined to make something work, you can. Undoubtedly you will come across points of your goal that might well be tough, and it will mean needing to learn.

As you journey toward achieving your goal, you will meet people, likeminded friends and work colleagues that can and will support you if you let them. Finding a mentor in an area you need support, is one great way to find a solution. Sometimes we have to learn the hard way, but learning means moving forward through trial and error. Sometimes we need to ask for help and use others knowledge, skill, and experience to advance us in our march to success.

Every journey is different. We are all individual, and no story is the same. But if we listen to our inner determination, we can achieve great things.

When you come up against difficulties, look for practical tools, solutions, method, and ideas to move forward. Usually, at some point, someone else has been there, where you are with the same problem and moved through it.

I love the saying 'we stand on the shoulders of giants' because, in truth, in life, that is all we ever do. We are lucky and privileged to be born into a time where so much has been done before us, for us.

Whatever you decide to do, whatever idea you choose to bring to the world, do it with love and let it be from a compassionate place because, as any good salesperson will tell you, selling value is easy. If you choose to add value to the world, solve a problem, make people happy, answer questions, be the product or service that support a challenge, if you choose to give, you ultimately receive.

I wish you all well in your onward journey and thank you for taking the time to read this book. I truly hope it has in some way resonated with you. If it has, please share it with your friends and family.

Share it on your Facebook, Twitter, and Instagram, whichever social media platforms you prefer and tag me in or send me a note. I'll be sure to re-tweet and re-post your kind comments, reviews and even photos of you with the book. Help me to spread this message and further positivity to others.

Find me on Twitter @pierrecoombes or Instagram @pierrecoombes. You can also check out my website

www.pierrecoombes.co.uk.

Thank you. Pierre Coombes.